QUES

YOU

SHOULD

BE ASKING

YOURSELF

?

AND ONLY YOU
CAN ANSWER

MIKE JONES

Questions You Should Be Asking Yourself

First published in 2020 by

Panoma Press Ltd
48 St Vincent Drive, St Albans, Herts, AL1 5SJ, UK
info@panomapress.com
www.panomapress.com

Book layout by Neil Coe.

978-1-784529-07-9

The right of Mike Jones to be identified as the author of this work has been asserted in accordance with sections 77 and 78 of the Copyright, Designs and Patents Act 1988.

A CIP catalogue record for this book is available from the British Library.

This book is available online and in bookstores.

DEDICATION

To Marisa, for keeping my feet on the floor and my
eye on the ball.

To Charlie, Ash and Mol – my three daughters and
so much more besides. You'll always be Daddy's
little girls and I'm proud of the women that you
have become.

ACKNOWLEDGEMENTS

Writing this book has been an amazingly cathartic exercise. For the last 12 months I've recalled countless experiences, encounters and emotions, and as I've done so I've been able to reflect on the eclectic mix of people that have either come and gone or entered and remained in my life. I hope that my own tales of fallibility enable you to remember your own, and the lessons that these moments have provided you with.

In this book you'll hear about many of the lead roles that have been by my side – my wife, my business partner and my best friend (that's one person not three). Being as opposite to me as it's possible to be, I've learned so much from her in terms of understanding and embracing my shadow.

You'll read about my girls – the blonde, brunette and redhead trio – who have provided me with so many opportunities to question, challenge and doubt myself in the way that only your children can. Then there's my mother, who makes the odd appearance in the ensuing pages. She brought up three children single-handed, teaching them her version of the difference between right and wrong, some of which (but not all) has rubbed off on her youngest.

In my early career I was fortunate enough to be led by some people at the forefront of my mind when I wrote this book, most notably Duncan Nield. He demonstrated that work should be fun, and if it's not, then go and do something that is. Thanks Duncan, I've been having fun for years! The single most defining moment of my career was meeting Insights, the Scottish-based Learning and Development company. As a customer, employee and now consultant, they were more than an employer should ever be. To Andi and Andy Lothian – thank you for everything. Ubuntu.

In order to achieve this goal, I am indebted to three people who have provided me with feedback throughout the journey – Inez Hogarth, Rebeka Graham and Amanda Sargent. Their unswerving support proved invaluable and spurred me on whenever I felt like pressing the pause button.

CONTENTS

OPENING

'That's a great question' – four of my favourite words that have ever been strung together into one sentence.

The pleasure I get when I receive that short response to a question that I have posed is pretty intense. Having never taken drugs I can only assume that this is what a high feels like. It's my legal high and I'm addicted to it.

I get paid to ask questions. As a facilitator and coach, I help individuals, teams and organisations gain clarity and momentum. It's my job and I love what I do. When my favourite response comes back ('that's a great question') and it's generally the quickest response that any question gets, it suggests to me that the person that it was asked of doesn't quite have an answer just yet. They need to stop, think and reflect before giving a considered response.

Over the course of this book I'm posing you 52 questions. Questions that when you first read them you don't necessarily have an immediate answer to, and if you did it wouldn't be the 'best' response, probably more of a reaction. If when you read the question you think to yourself 'that's a great question – I wish I had a great answer' then you're in luck! By the time you've read the chapter relating to the title question and subsequently reflected on it for a while, making notes as you go, I reckon you'll arrive at a great answer. Your answer.

An answer that provides you with clarity on what is important, who is important and what steps you should be taking for your benefit and the benefit of those people whose opinions and lives matter to you.

Well, I say 52 – that's how many questions there are in the chapter titles. Actually, over the next 200 or so pages there are approximately

700 – that's around 14 per chapter. I told you questions were important to me.

The questions that you will be asked, then subsequently answer, are a wide and varied bunch. Let's face it, you'd soon get bored if you had to answer the same question 52 times. There are questions about your relationships – those that are in good shape and those that might require a few changes. There are some that are aimed at increasing self-awareness and others focused on self-worth. There's a combination of those related more to your professional life compared to those that focus more on your personal life, whereas others galvanise you to look at both as you consider how you might achieve more balance, whatever balance looks like for you. This highlights a key point: for all of the questions that you are about to mull over there is no right or wrong answer.

I'll share some of my own stories with you, not because I have the answer to the question, but because when writing this book I've been answering my own questions as I've gone along. As I've done this my own memories, emotions and experiences have come flooding back. I've smiled, I've laughed and I've shed the odd tear as I've captured them, reflecting on the people that have accompanied me on my adventure, many of whom I had forgotten about until they were brought back into consciousness. You'll do the same, and you'll be surprised what you recall. It's been a roller coaster ride for the author I can tell you, and I want you to hop on to that very same roller coaster. Strap yourself in and enjoy the ride!

The questions will ask you to consider the past, analyse the present and look to the future as you spend time on the one person who will always be there in your life – you. If that's a scary thought, then we need to spend a little bit of time ensuring that you like that person – and that's in the upcoming pages too.

I want you to get greater clarity – clarity on who you are, what you do, why you do it and who you choose to do it with. Clarity on where you've been, where you are and where you're going. It's your journey after all, so it would be so much simpler if the map was a little easier to read.

This book is meant for you, and your timing for choosing to read it is perfect. There's no niche market, and there's no optimum time, and I'm not just saying that because I want as many people as possible to buy the book. Trust me? It's important that we establish a bit of trust if we're to go on this journey together!

Whatever stage of life that you find yourself in, and however successful or unsuccessful you currently claim to be, arriving at answers will help you move to the next stage with greater desire, determination and optimism. I really do believe that.

My suggestion is that you don't read this like the novel that accompanied you on your last holiday and you devoured in the space of a few hours. Even if that is your intention I bet you that it won't happen. There's way too much to reflect on for you to take that approach. I've created one question for each week of the year and it might take you that long to get through them all (and it might not). Then again, I set myself a target of writing one chapter a week, completing the book in 12 months as a result, and got ahead of myself as my excitement and momentum grew in tandem. The same might happen to you but try not to rush it – in doing so you might just gloss over the very question that is most significant to you at that point in time.

Right then, I reckon it's time for you to get started, you've got a lot to answer for. I've not got your answers and neither has anyone else. It's over to you. Are you ready? There you go, that was an easy one to get you started…

1. WHO SEES THE BEST POSSIBLE VERSION OF YOU AND WHO WOULD BENEFIT FROM SEEING A BETTER VERSION?

My dog thinks I'm pretty special; I can do no wrong in her eyes. Yet, as Ann Landers the American columnist said, "Don't accept your dog's admiration as conclusive evidence that you are wonderful."

The unconditional love of a dog, or a parent for that matter, is the exception rather than the norm. Not everyone thinks the sun shines from the same location as those that love you most. For everyone else we need to work at it, to provide evidence of what makes us the special person that we are.

Consider what you look like when you are at your best. When the sun is shining, your team is winning and business is booming it's easy to show off your best bits. So what are those behaviours that rise to the surface and reveal themselves in all their finery?

What are those strengths that perhaps aren't on show every day of the week yet happen to reveal themselves for certain people? What is it about their behaviour that has the ability to coax them out of hibernation and show that side of you that you like the most and gain most benefit from? Sometimes those people who you wish would be the welcome recipients of such positive behaviour rarely gain access to it. Whether it be your boss, your customer, your partner or one of your little ones, it's often them that bear the brunt of your bad day behaviours.

Who would benefit from seeing a better version of you? What are those behaviours that they witness that you would prefer to remove from your repertoire?

As you reflect on those that benefit from the best possible version of you, it's worth considering the relationship that you have with them and the topics that you tend to discuss. What are those interactions that bring out the positive side of the coin? What are you talking about when you are in the zone, where you appear most assured, most passionate or most on purpose?

Are the people who see the best version of you those that you care about the most? Is the best version saved for the closest people or is it spent on those that see you less frequently or who only spend time talking to you on specific topics?

How would those that see the good day behaviour describe you? What are you actually doing or saying or thinking when those desirable qualities emerge? Whether it be your engaging *joie de vivre*, or your objective critical thinking, how can you capture and bottle it so that it can be savoured by the wider circles you mix in?

I work with many people who say they are quite different in their professional and personal lives, with those sharing their meeting room and dining room exposed to a different set of emotions, words and actions. Yet quite often, if you were to put those who know you best in both formats in a room together to discuss the version of you that they see, the similarities will far outweigh the differences.

Sometimes, the fact that we are putting effort into being more or doing more of something makes us believe that we have become that 'something'. When I put effort into being quiet, it doesn't make me quiet. Where are you putting your effort and energy at the moment? Which behaviours are you trying to dial-up or dial-down, and for whose benefit? How would those that you live with describe you compared to those that you work with, and which of those two lists do you prefer?

Now focus in on the workplace. What is currently taking place there that seems to irritate or aggravate you? Who tends to be involved in those moments, and how does it impact on the behaviours that you exhibit? What is it about their own behaviour that acts as a catalyst for yours?

As you focus on the key question to be answered, reflect on how similar to or how different from you the other person is. It's easy to understand the behaviours of those that are like us, and because they are like us, we often like them. When looking to fill vacancies we often look for those that are like us. Often however, interactions with these types can be akin to a bird pecking itself in the mirror. Projection often rears its head where those traits that we find irritating in others are found within ourselves. Any bells ringing as you reflect on your relationships at this point?

When I joined my last employer, I began on the same day as another guy and my first impressions were not positive. I perceived him to be an arrogant know-all who seemingly enjoyed the sound of his own voice more than those forced to listen to it did, including me. Imagine my horror the day after, when we shared the results of a behavioural preference assessment and our scores were exactly the same. Was I describing myself in the undesirable combination of traits that I laid at his door? This experience was over 20 years ago and it still serves as a sense check when I feel myself getting irritated by the posturing of others.

Now what about those folk that are opposite to you – the night to your day? How valuing are you of those differences? What aspects of their behaviours stimulate a reaction in you that subsequently spills out in what you say and do? Where might you need to be more valuing of others, and if you were how might it impact your own behaviour?

If the person that sees the best version of you had a chat with the person that doesn't, how would that conversation go? What could the latter learn from the former, and what could you learn from them both? Would they have ever met before? Do they mix in the same circles? Would they each recognise the person that the other was describing? It's all you – the same heart, the same head and the same voice – even if it might sound like a different beast altogether.

By the way, which one do you see? Now I bet that's opened up a whole new can of worms!

2. WHAT QUESTION ARE YOU PUTTING OFF ASKING OR ANSWERING?

Procrastination hey, we're all at it. I'll tell you why later. Whether it be renewing our physical vows at the gym or giving that developmental feedback that might not be so welcome to the recipient, we are all guilty of putting stuff on the back burner, and then leaving it there.

You'll have gathered by now that I love questions, and by my reckoning so do you otherwise you wouldn't be reading this book. If you ask me, a great question is one that requires you to reflect, but reflection and action don't have to be mutually exclusive. If the time spent in reflection doesn't result in some form of response, then you should be asking yourself questions. You see, they're everywhere! Or maybe, you're not responding because you don't like the answer that you know is waiting to be delivered. Maybe the answer serves as a wake-up call to you in regard to how you're spending your time and who you're spending it with.

Are the questions that you are struggling to answer challenging you because the response takes you out of your comfort zone? Yes or no? That's a simple closed question for you, merely requiring a one-word answer. How about a more expansive open question beginning with a who, what, why, when, where or how? Which one challenges you the most? Which – now there's another to add to the list.

Those 'why' questions can sometimes be a tad punitive don't you think? Where the poser of the question has already decided that the course of action taken wasn't one that they fully concur with. A question such as 'Why did you do that?' can immediately put us on the defensive, yet the 'why' question can be powerful, helping us get to the root cause of an issue. Ask yourself 'why' six times in a row and the chances are that you'll get to the heart of an issue. A word of caution however, ask it to others and you might get a clip round the ear!

Asking yourself 'why' can really help you establish the purpose behind a task, galvanising those seeking to accomplish it to gain clarity on the whole reason for doing so. It can be the difference between painting lines on a road and making the world a safer place. Let's not spend all our time on that particular starter for ten though. Who needs your help? What do you need to do differently? When are you going to make that call? How will you resolve the issue? Where should you be? Your question may well not be any of those, so if it's not them, what is it? What is that question that you are putting off asking yourself, or answering?

Einstein once said, "The important thing is to never stop questioning." Some, however, see questions as a form of interrogation and prefer not to go down the Einstein route, even though it didn't do him any harm. If that's you then perhaps you should change your paradigm and look for the positive intent behind a question. Consider that when someone questions others they are showing curiosity, interest and a desire to see things from a different perspective, and when they question themselves they are challenging themselves or seeking confirmation that they are on the right road.

Right now you're probably looking for examples where this optimistic collection doesn't quite fit and there are always exceptions to rules. At school we learned that it was I before E except after C

– well let me tell you, my foreign neighbour's feisty eight-year-old son, Keith, thought that was weird. If you didn't count six in that lot, go back and read again!

Of course, the question that you are holding fire on might not be aimed at you. If that is the case, who is the intended target? Who do you need to speak to in order to understand that issue currently festering in the workplace? Within the confines of your own four homely walls, who do you need to connect with to get under the surface of a developing story? Consider how, by saying the previously unsaid, it might move you and them forward.

To date, it's been assumed that the question master is you, but the world is full of question masters and your world is densely populated with people seeking clarity from you or awaiting your opinion. When teaching from the front of a classroom it's deemed acceptable to respond to a question with 'good question, I don't know. I'll find out and get back to you'. It might suit the teacher-pupil interaction but the rest of us can't resort to this escape route on too many occasions without being challenged to change our approach.

Who is currently waiting for you to 'find out and get back to them'? Who are you leaving on the end of the proverbial line? Is the other person getting false hope by not being delivered the message that you know you need to deliver but are either unable or unwilling to?

Now I'm not trying to coerce you into transforming every sentence that comes out of your mouth so that it ends in a question mark, but what I am striving for is to get you to consider the impact of asking the question and the consequences of not. For every effect there's a cause, and for every movement towards something there's a compensatory movement away from something else. Or looking at it from a different angle, for every answer there's a question. If you want curly hair you need to eat your crusts (or so my grandmother used to say); if you want good eyesight you need to eat your carrots; and if you want to arrive at the answer you need to ask the question.

I can only assume that, like me, your desire for good eyesight is stronger than your desire for curly hair, but let's put carrots, curls and old wives' tales to one side and focus on answers. Answers provide solutions, solutions provide breakthroughs and breakthroughs lead to progress.

So, what question are you putting off asking or answering that could lead to personal or professional breakthroughs for you and yours? Now there's a question.

3. WHAT NEGATIVE EMOTION DO YOU NEED TO LET GO OF?

Shortly after we all stopped concerning ourselves with the millennium bug, my life took a dramatic turn for the worse. I'm not going to fill these pages with the ins and outs of the whys and hows, but let's just say that the decisions I'd made had led me to a dark place of loneliness, with a relationship that meant the world to me and more tossed on the scrapheap. My emotions and business performance were at an all-time low with my mind all consumed with 'what ifs?', yearning to move the clock back weeks and months so that decisions could be remade with a different set of results.

I tried, sometimes successfully and other times less so, to focus on the day job of facilitating workshops on all the topics that had failed me in my own life – cultivating relationships, taking responsibility and decision making. Each time I got up to speak to the paying client it led me to question whether I was just a personal development fraud.

Then something happened that enabled my professional life to have a profound effect on its personal counterpart. I was co-facilitating a session with a colleague and he was keen to incorporate a new activity into our workshop during one of the evenings of the residential programme and, having agreed to it, my intrigue grew as a canister of helium gas was carried into the room. The session in question focused on negative emotions, and asked us to consider which ones held us back. Together we created a comprehensive list of such emotions – anger, resentment, jealousy and blame all coming together – and as the list grew, my own millstone around my neck became abundantly clear to me. I was riddled with regret.

As an exercise, we each wrote our negative emotion on a piece of card, tied it to a balloon filled with helium, and then stepped out into the night sky. One by one (a few years before the world belatedly became more aware of our responsibilities to the birds that shared the sky), we released them. For me it was an intensely cathartic exercise and one that has shaped my approach to life, love and letting go of the past ever since. I'm no Edith Piaf but I like to think she'd be mildly impressed with her kindred spirit.

What negative emotion do you need to let go of? What word would rise up, up and away if you were to relinquish your grip on your balloon? What are you guilty of that you shouldn't be? Who do you spend unnecessary time being jealous of rather than appreciating what you have? When does your passion spill over into an angry side of you that is neither attractive nor productive? And instead of blaming something, someone, everything or everyone for your plight, what could you do to take more responsibility?

Consider the last 24 hours of your life, and the emotions that have been expressed during that time. The chances are that you will have displayed a whole gamut of them – the good, the bad and the ugly. If you could turn the clock back, are there any that you wish you hadn't displayed (not that I'm advocating regret you understand!)? Consider the conversations you've had and how you might have reacted to someone else's words or actions.

Now work on the premise that you and you alone are responsible for your own emotional reactions. Your frustrated outburst after someone had the temerity to say the wrong thing at the wrong time, that was your choice. Oh, and your 'why does it always rain on me?' bout of self-pity – you selected that option too. Empower yourself by taking charge of your own feelings and you'll be taking a step closer to releasing your blame balloon.

The reality is that there is a time and a place for negative emotions. If someone breaks into your house and violates your privacy and property, it would be ridiculous to think that anger wouldn't accompany the action. If you're in a road accident when the other person shot out of a T-Junction and bumped into you whilst you were driving just fine, then it would be wholly appropriate to blame the other person for the damage caused. We're talking about those emotions that wear you down and hold you back from getting as much fulfilment from your time on this earth as possible. The ones that leave you feeling guilty about the choices you did or didn't make, getting frustrated by the small, insignificant things and then stacking them on top of each other so that they come crashing down all around you, causing you to ask those most defeatist of questions: 'why do I bother?' or 'why me?'.

Why do you bother? Go on, why do you? If it just makes you angry or resentful, jealous or riddled with regret, then what's the point? Which negative emotion would you benefit from being free of, and by doing so, create time and space to be filled with all those positive emotions? Where could you express more joy? What is currently giving you hope? What are you grateful for and who would benefit from you showing it? How could you create space for a splash of serenity? Answer yourself those questions and you may have got a step or four closer to responding to the first one.

So, grab a pen, scribble down your thoughts, and see what emerges for you as you aim to identify that one negative emotion more than any other that you need to let go of. What are the memories that you can think of, similar to but different from my own reflections referred to earlier, that might help to unearth the word that you should be writing down? Don't worry though, you don't need to head out to the gas shop, the helium was an optional extra that I haven't used since. Not that my ex-colleague knows that − I wouldn't want to burst his balloon.

4. IF YOU WERE TO DECLUTTER YOUR LIFE WHAT WOULD YOU THROW OUT?

How often do you throw the bag away that drops through your letter box without giving it a second glance – the one that requests you to place all your unwanted items of this, that and a bit of the other into it, in the name of charity? One such charity in the UK aimed at helping the elderly has recently conducted research into why so many of these bags get cast aside without giving consideration as to what we can easily and readily dispose of, and by doing so generating much needed revenue for the variety of good causes. The results show that this small island of ours is becoming a nation of hoarders, seemingly unwilling or unable to be parted from all the 'collateral' collected over the years.

The most recent bag that landed on our doormat requested any unwanted (or unfitting!) clothing, shoes, toys, CDs and bric-a-brac. Do you know what bric-a-brac is? Me neither, so I've just looked it up on the internet and the response was 'miscellaneous objects of little value' – so there you have it. They want us to declutter our wardrobe, drawers, garages and attics of all the objects, garments and treasures that in reality no longer hold any value to us.

Now if that doesn't have you frantically searching for the last bag that remained empty, nothing will! Or maybe it won't, because there's a part of us that wants to hold on to our possessions, regardless of how much or how little value they are seen to add. Take a peek in your wardrobe – as you look at each garment, reflect on the last time that you actually wore it. Any that you haven't worn in the last 12 months, or beyond? What are you doing – saving it for a special occasion?

Now head to the kitchen. Aside from all those gadgets that populate the surfaces, how many jars are behind closed doors that last saw the light of day when the only place you could find a recipe was in a cookery book? While you're there, check out those use-by dates and empty your shelves of all the golden oldies. A point of clarity might be needed here – these should not be placed in the charity bag! Now this is nice and simple isn't it – a chance to give your home a spring clean, creating the space for the next onset of purchases, ensuring that the same exercise can be repeated in the next decade.

Let's up the ante then and cast our net a bit wider than the contents of your refrigerator. Consider how you are spending your time and who you're spending it with. Reflect on the thoughts that run through your mind, the inner voice that scurries unabated on the hamster wheel of your life. What thoughts would you benefit from removing from your mind? What conversations that remain within would you benefit from expunging? Who are you spending time with where the time, effort and energy are collectively way in excess of the benefit gained? What are you spending time doing, and where are you going, that if you were to claw that time back it could be invested in a more fulfilling manner? If you were to declutter your life what could, would or should you throw out?

Social media has had an impact on the way that we live our lives in so many ways, and it too might benefit from a review while you're in the middle of getting rid of your unwanted baggage. Through the continuous use of Facebook, Instagram, Twitter and the rest, we've begun to measure success by the number of friends and followers we have. The number of likes, loves and comments we receive provides us with our popularity fix and who cares if people we've never even met are fawning all over us with their birthday wishes? Are you glancing at how many friends others have and beating yourself up for lagging so far behind?

Why not, instead of surfing and snooping at others' pages, contemplating who to add to give your ego a quick-fire massage, go the other way? Who can you delete or unfollow, and in turn, declutter your online world in order to focus on those people that actually matter? How often do you get frustrated by the comments of those people that just don't mean that much to you? Why let them in? They're like alcoholic calories, contributing nothing to your diet. Or why not go the whole hog and remove some of those apps that take up some of your time (let alone space on your smartphone) yet never really add value to your day?

Before you start living in a shell, devoid of any trace of how you've lived your life past and present, I'm not suggesting that decluttering means removing all and sundry. If you're a gardener you will trim your favourite plants back at certain times of the year to enable them to return bigger, bolder and more colourful than they were before, so think of this whole chapter as pruning back your shrubs. What weeds do you need to pull out to allow those most vibrant plants to blossom?

If you were to calculate how much time you spend with all the people who comprise your network, it might make for interesting reading. In fact, let's do this for a moment, and I want you to think of a jar (one of those ones that you didn't throw out) made up of three ingredients: rocks, stones and sand. Think of those that you love the most, and where that love is reciprocated. Time spent with them is precious for all parties – view these people as the rocks. Moving on to the stones, these are those productive relationships that are mutually beneficial. The stones will find a way into the jar by seeking out the spaces left behind by the rocks. Finally, pour in the sand. The sand is everyone else – not the loved, not the productive – the others. Those interactions you have that fill your time but not your heart.

We all have these types of interactions of course, and as long as you put the rocks in first, followed by the stones then the sand, it's all good. But what happens if the sand gets poured in first – you try getting your stones in then, and how on earth do the rocks find a place? Are your priorities right? Are you making the space for those that matter most? If not, then how might some decluttering help you? Is all that sand absolutely necessary? I think you probably know the answer by now so don't bury your head in it.

5. WHAT DO YOU WANT TO BE REMEMBERED FOR?

On reading the title question, you may have suddenly gone to a sombre place with thoughts of death, who might show up at your funeral and the words that might emanate from the eulogy. That's not where this question is going though, unless you specifically want it to, that is.

You can expand and complete this question in so many ways by adding a plethora of endings. What do you want to be remembered for when you've left your company, left the room, left the team, left the conversation or left the relationship? So put the Will writing to one side just for the moment, and consider the difference that you want to make to your world and those who are touched, however fleetingly, by your presence, because every time we say something, make an expression, or press send on an email, we have the opportunity to make a difference.

Think of the people that you met yesterday and the conversations that took place. Can you remember what you said? Were you positive? Were you valuing? Were you fair? That's just three to consider for now, and some of them might be more important to you than others. I'm not saying they are the most important three though, so what is important to you? Would you prefer to be remembered for being fearless more than fair, vibrant more than valuing, or productive more than positive?

Now consider the last meeting that you were a part of. As you left the room, how would you want people to describe the difference that you made to proceedings? How did they feel? What conversations might they be having about the impact your words, actions and behaviour had on the group dynamics and on them as individuals? Sometimes these interactions are fleeting; we've all been told that you only get one chance to make a first impression, and when people enter your world at one station and alight at the next, that first impression could well be the only one they get.

Imagine then, when this character is subsequently asked 'have you ever met John Brown?' and their answer is 'yeah, he was a bit aloof if I recall'. What exactly will they recall? As Maya Angelou said, "People will forget what you said, people will forget what you did, but people will never forget how you made them feel." So if we work on that premise, let's focus on the feelings that you leave behind long after you've departed. How would you like people to feel having spent time in your company?

Think about your commercial environment for a moment. Remember your first boss – how did they make you feel? I'm thinking of two of my earliest leaders as I type, and whereas one made me feel important and worthwhile, the other was sparing in her praise and gushing in her criticism. I recollect them both clearly and I've not seen either of them for over 30 years. They might not remember me, but I sure remember them – and if they're reading this book, hi!

Do you want to be remembered for being great fun, a good listener, someone who asked great questions, or someone who got things done and made things happen? Maybe you would like to be remembered as having a strategic mind, being creative and innovative, having a big heart or being kind. Do some or all of these resonate with you? The list is endless and the list is yours.

Would you want those that you meet for the first time next week to have the same thoughts and feelings as those that met you the day you collected your first pay packet? Now compare the list of what you would like to be remembered for and what you would actually be remembered for. Similar or different? What steps might you need to take to move from actual to desired? They say the best time to plant a tree is 20 years ago, the second best time is now. You can't change what you were remembered for way back when, but the second best time to make that change is now. What are those behaviours that you need to add to your portfolio and which ones might you seek to reduce or remove?

When a relationship develops over a sustained period of time, those initial perceptions can alter, and at times drastically change. We have more opportunities to make a difference and they have more information to work with. How might your impact be different if individuals get the opportunity to spend more time with you. 'Actually he's a decent guy once you get to know him.' How long do people actually need with you in order to see the stuff that you want them to see?

Think of all the roles that you perform in your world – those roles that you perform in your family, your clubs, your communities. Consider how many teams that you are a part of in the workplace. Reflect on each and every relationship that you have that matters to you. What will you be remembered for in each of those aspects of your world – as a parent, as a friend, as a customer, supplier, leader, captain, colleague, coach, mentor or life partner. When we stop and think about it for a while, we don't half make a difference to a lot of people, and we'll be remembered. The choice is yours as to whether those memories will be recalled as a breath of fresh air or with a bitter taste in the mouth.

As you create your own list of the various roles that you play (not all ten that I listed will apply), consider which ones are most in need of action if you are to be remembered by that person or those people in the way that you would like. What do you need to stop, start and continue doing to leave your legacy of choice with your network? Where there's a will there's a way. Oh hang on, I said we weren't writing one of those…

6. WHAT DO YOU NEED TO START MEASURING SO YOU CAN MAKE IMPROVEMENTS?

Some of us like a good stat more than others and I recognise that I most definitely fit into the 'more' category. I'm probably off the scale on this one as I tend to measure everything. When I'm on the treadmill I know throughout my stint what percentage has passed and therefore how much remains. The bracelet on my arm measures every step that I take, and on car journeys the length and breadth of the country, the dashboard is my permanent companion with its array of numbers and metrics to keep me entertained along the way.

Granted, some of my measurements are more for my own analytical pleasure rather than to ascertain progress (studies show that stepping on to the scales can do more harm than good), but I have both feet firmly in the Peter Drucker camp, fully concurring when he stated, "What gets measured gets managed" to widespread agreement in the business world.

So think for a minute about what you currently measure and what information, benefit, and besides that, pleasure, you get from doing so? From finance to fitness, and waste reduction to waist reduction how do the numbers that you keep tabs on enable you to compare where you've been with where you are, casting one eye on where you want to get to? Where in your life would you like to see improvement, and how will you measure that improvement? Let's take the ongoing battle that we are all faced with – the one that we refer to as work-life balance. Just think of all the ways in which this thorny subject could be evaluated.

First of all, let's agree that 'balance' in this area is a subjective word – what constitutes balance to one is disparity to another. Recently I spoke at a conference where this subject arose and I asked the audience how many of them felt that they had effective balance in this area, and approximately one third of them raised their hands. My second question, "How many of you think you need to spend more time focusing on work?" was met with stillness followed by laughter at the very thought. So two thirds of the audience believed that they needed to focus more on the component of the equation called 'life', yet were seemingly waiting for someone else to create it for them.

Consider these five questions on the subject. How many days' holiday did you have last year compared to the previous five years? How many hours are you spending in your place of work a week and how does that compare to what you think would equate to balance? How many days/nights out are you having with loved ones? How much time are you spending on your favourite hobby? What time are you going to bed each evening?

Acquiring such information can only help you make the choices that will make the difference and lead to more time off, fewer hours in the workplace, more time with the people that matter, doing the things that mean most to you, and more time resting and recuperating so that you can go again with renewed vigour.

Think of the pleasure that measurement has provided you with over the years, making comparisons between yesterday and yesteryear. Peel away the wallpaper from the walls and the chances are that you'll find markings showing how the little members of the family became not so little in the blink of an eye. The gradual increase in height of the pencil line provides a warm and fuzzy nostalgia in both those who made the mark and those who stood straight as an arrow in their quest to add any millimetre that they could muster.

These captured moments in time measure progress, but aside from purchasing a bigger pair of heels there wasn't much that you could do to impact future markings. The same cannot be said for other aspects of your world where a first measurement could lead to enhancements to your daily lot.

Ever wonder how your money mysteriously evaporates from your bank account? Concerned that your alcohol intake might be more than is deemed healthy? Anxious that you're not going to finish writing a book in time for the publisher's deadline? OK, I thought I'd throw in one of my own to help you along with your own list!

What do you need to start measuring so that you can make improvements in that aspect of your life – your work life, family life, your health or your finances? Athletes the world over are setting personal bests, and the only way that they know they've beaten it is to measure – the previous, the current and the future. Where are you ready, wanting or needing to beat a personal best at the moment, and what is your current personal best? If you don't know it then measure it, and hey presto, you'll have a personal best. The highest, lightest, furthest, deepest, longest, wealthiest, healthiest. What 'est' are you wanting to create so that you can then embark on passing it?

Apparently, one of the most commonly asked questions in interviews is 'how do you measure success?' That's a great question – not dissimilar to one you'll find elsewhere in this book. The reality is that when answering that question people will actually respond to a related yet different question: 'how do you define success?' Spot the difference?

The latter is easier to answer – most of us can daydream about what an ideal world looks like, picturing what we are doing, where and with whom. How do you measure it? Well that requires us to be able to identify at any given time how we are doing compared to that response. The good news if you are heading for an interview sometime soon and don't have an answer is that in most cases the interviewer doesn't know the difference between the two either.

So do yourself a favour and get ahead of the game – define it, measure it, then set about inching yourself closer to the holy grail. And while you've got your tape measure out, just check to see if you've grown or shrunk in the last 12 months – you might be surprised!

7. WHAT CAN YOU LEARN FROM THE PERSON YOU REALLY SEEM TO STRUGGLE WITH?

Think of all those people that you interact with – in the office, in your social circles and in your home; the conversations that we have, however brief, that comprise our day. Aren't we lucky that everyone we come into contact with in these contrasting aspects of our world uplifts us, leaving us in a better place than before they opened their mouth? If only we lived in that kind of world! The reality is that we are all challenged by someone and that someone is more often than not someone who doesn't tend to go away!

Think for a moment. What behaviour is it that you find most difficult to connect with? Look back on your adult life, in fact go back as far as you like. Who are your monsters – those people that, try as hard as you might, you just seemed to struggle to make a productive connection with? In fact, every time they had the temerity to open their mouth you thought it was with the sole intention to make your life more difficult, more awkward or just more damn miserable!

If you could describe that person and their behaviour in one word what would that word be? Is it the aggressive person, or negative perhaps? How about the moaner or the manipulator? Let's add in a few more to the party. The backstabber, the lazy one and the disingenuous one walked into a bar. Except it's no joke when these behaviours cause the reaction that they do in you, leaving you feeling like it's a personal attack designed to remove all your positivity and sense of goodwill to all men and women.

Now that we've been able to reflect on who our monsters have been over the years, let me ask you another question: whose monster are you? Who would find your behaviour difficult to connect with, and what is it that you say and do that would cause a negative paradigm in others? What could these people learn from you and vice versa? For difficult behaviour we can often replace that word with one that starts off in the same direction but then takes a disarming turn. Try changing the word difficult to different.

Stephen Covey taught the world the seven habits of highly effective people, and in doing so brought to the surface the mindset that behind every behaviour there is a positive intention. This works wonders when trying to see some light at the end of our relationship tunnels. Now consider that monstrous set of behaviours that you created a few minutes ago. What do you think might be the positive intention behind some of those? How might you change the way that you look at it?

Take the aggressor – are they being aggressive or are they just conveying passion? What was the positive intention behind the behaviour? Were they looking to create a greater sense of urgency, or challenging the status quo? Is that person that you purport to being a negative killjoy actually demonstrating an ability to look at issues with a critical eye, designed to reach a higher level of quality? Why accept second best? How does that pragmatic reality check serve to help you and others?

Carl Jung said, "Everything that irritates us about others can lead us to a greater understanding of ourselves." That's my favourite quote from the great man, and there's plenty to quote believe me! So what can you learn about yourself by the way that you tend to react to the behaviour of the person that you struggle with? Why do you react the way you do when, as you look around you, others don't seem to be quite so contorted with the same angst?

Does your own behaviour contribute in any way to the behaviour that you observe in them? What words emerge from your mouth that might act as a catalyst to the responding ones that are discharged from theirs?

For every effect there's a cause. Could that cause be you? If you're sitting there shaking your head at this point, then consider what behaviour you would like them to display. How might you contribute to this desired state? If you want someone to smile more, how about a compliment, an amusing anecdote or recalling a mutually agreeable moment from the past? If you want someone to contribute more in a meeting, try adding items to the agenda that you know they are interested in, asking the odd open question in their direction, or creating an environment conducive to healthy debate.

Now consider what components of their behaviour you would like to add to your own repertoire. Fancy a bit more drive? Would you like to create a buzz in any room that you walk into? Would a tad more empathy not go amiss? Would you like to remember a few more facts and figures than you currently seem capable of?

Take time to observe your nemesis for a while. Keep an eye on their behaviour in conversations with others and spot the clues that they (and the rest of us) are displaying on a continual basis. The best way to acquire a new desired behaviour is to act as if you have it. Want to be more positive? Well how about saying something positive! Want to show more urgency? Well do stuff quicker. What do they do that you could replicate and amalgamate with your existing behaviours so that, whilst it might look aligned to theirs in isolation, will look unmistakeably yours when it is stirred in with the other ingredients already in your pan?

People can be so frustrating don't you think? Their foibles and idiosyncrasies, their warts and all. But what if we could turn that frustration into fascination? When we are fascinated about something we seek to understand what lies behind the surface, we spend more time getting clarity on the full picture, rather than filling in all of the gaps to create our own story. Try being fascinated with that person you really seem to struggle with, and who knows, you might just learn something from them.

8. WHAT DO YOU NEED TO KEEP TELLING YOURSELF?

In the previous chapter I asked you who your monsters were — those people that you struggle to make a connection with. Whilst writing, as each chapter has come to a conclusion I've forwarded it to a select few people who I can rely on for a combination of honest feedback and encouraging words. As they've reviewed them they've also done exactly what I wanted — considered their own responses to each question. It seems that the most popular response when asked 'which person do you most seem to struggle with' was themselves. I must admit that when I was writing the words to accompany that question, I wasn't anticipating that response, but hey, there are no wrong answers in this book!

So often we're our own biggest critic, beating ourselves up before anyone else gets a chance to land a punch. When I was in my lowest days, feeling unloved and unworthy, a colleague and friend gave me a book to read, written by Peter McWilliams, and I struggled to get past the title: *Love 101: To Love Oneself is the Beginning of a Lifelong Romance*. Yet eventually I did manage to turn the pages, slowly at first then increasingly faster as the subject struck home. The abiding message that I took away was how difficult it is to truly love someone else if you don't love yourself. Do you love yourself? If so, why, and if not, why not?

Think of that inner voice of yours – friend or foe? Biggest advocate or biggest critic? If it's the latter of both of those pairings then you're not alone. Full of self-limiting beliefs and self-deprecating assessments of your performance, when it's pecking away it can feel like the grit in your oyster and the dog poo on your shoe. Getting it to scarper isn't so easy but diluting it is. Like pouring white wine on the stain of its red counterpart, populating your mind with encouragement, acknowledgement and praise will serve to reduce the impact of the less desirable stuff.

What do you need to keep telling yourself and how will you benefit as a result? Do any of these fit for you? You can do it. You are good enough. You are worth it. You deserve it. Or how about this one: you are a good person. That one brings back warm fuzzy memories of when I first started dating my wife. When some others were proving themselves to be challenging adversaries, in danger of derailing my road to relationship recovery, she would look me in the eye and state with great certainty those very four words: "You're a good person." If you hear something often enough, you believe it.

Think back to what you've been called in the past and the insults seem to stick with us more than the accolades. Don't wallow in that place of reflection for too long though, as I'd much prefer you replace it with a more affirmative statement. Because after I heard Marisa tell me these words so many times she no longer had to say them. I knew them. I knew she thought it and I knew that I did too.

Let me tell you now, while it's on your mind – you most definitely are worth it, you do deserve it, you are good enough and a mighty fine person to boot (even the most hardened of criminals have the potential to be). And while I'm on a roll, you're not too old, too fat, too tired, too anything. Go and stick your negative self-talk somewhere that it can't be found again; it's just noisy clutter that helps nothing and hinders everything.

Consider the various roles that you perform. What do you need to keep telling yourself in your role of spouse, parent, boss, or committee member? Each of them requires something different from us and as they all blend into one in our hectic schedules it can feel like we're taking our foot off the pedal or eye off the ball in one, more, or all of them. Remind yourself why you perform that role, the pleasures that it presents and the gifts that you bring to the table. Remind yourself, then keep on reminding yourself until you don't lose sight of these reasons. Are you the right person for the role? In most cases I suspect the answer will be an unequivocal yes – just see what would happen and how you would react if someone tried to replace you.

You're nobody's one trick pony; those different versions of you might have some similarities, those indelible attributes that you take with you wherever you go, but they also require something different, even unique. Ensure that your new found positive inner voice covers the whole spectrum. You're a good mother because; you're the best person to do the job you do because; you're worth listening to in that meeting because; you can smash that goal because. I'll stop there but you don't have to – it's your voice and it's your words and I want to ignite the process not truncate it. The 'because' word is important as it's the suffix that makes what follows it a personal conversation between you and, er... you! Talking about yourself incessantly in social circles might be frowned on, but no such rules apply when those words can't be heard by anyone except yourself.

It's rare for most of us that the silence on the outside is mirrored on the inside, so if there is an internal dialogue taking place, far more beneficial don't you think if it makes the version of you that others are privy to a more positive, productive and polished version? If we're lucky, as I was, someone else will remind us of the value that we bring to the world and our right to be there in the first place.

Yet we shouldn't come to rely on it. The only person that is always there in your world is you. A bit of a pain in the butt then if you don't like that person.

So be kind to yourself, make friends with the enemy within. Keep telling yourself that actually you're not so bad after all. In fact, you're better than that, much better. You're a good person, and if you don't believe me, ask your version of Marisa.

9. WHAT ARE YOU LOOKING FORWARD TO MOST RIGHT NOW?

Please don't wish your life away. Whatever your beliefs are for when we leave this planet, just remember that we've all been lucky enough to have a life on earth but only for a finite amount of time. Every second counts and provides us with opportunities, so don't get my dander up by posting your Christmas countdown clock on social media the minute summer turns to autumn! That's not what I'm referring to here, but just know that there is so much to look forward to when you stop to give it some consideration. I'm writing these words in November, and without sounding like a hypocrite Christmas is most definitely on my list, but it's a long, eclectic list comprising goals, journeys, nights out, business adventures and time spent with people who make a positive difference to my world. That's not a bad bunch of five to act as a framework as you take time to consider what you are looking forward to most right now.

What are you looking forward to later today? How about the rest of this week? Is the upcoming weekend looking promising, and what about next month? Don't go all maudlin on me if you can't think of anything now will you? A part of asking you this question isn't just so you can remind yourself how wonderful your life is right now (and I really hope that is how you feel), it's so you can start filling in the blanks with moments that will enable you to get through the duller times, safe in the knowledge that pleasures in one guise or another are around the corner.

Let's start with the small stuff that might remind you that you're one of the lucky ones. Are you looking forward to getting in the bath for a good soak later? Is the thought of watching the final episode in that latest drama that has had you gripped getting you excited? Or is it getting some proper time with those people that share your home that's doing the trick? How often we are reminded that 'it's the little things that count'. If you tend to pour scorn on such throwaway comments let me remind you that the biggest killer in the world is the mosquito, and you don't see many giant versions of the little blighters, so the little things really can make a difference to our day and our frame of mind. Remind yourself what those small things are for you in the next ten hours. Don't read on until you've reached ten, and if you can't think of ten then you're setting your bar too high.

Then there's the whoppers – those events that make you giddy just thinking about them. They've been in the diary for an age, and when arranged, appeared to be so far in the future that it felt like they would never materialise. Yet the one thing you can be sure that never stops is the relentless march of time. The sense of excitement leading up to them is enough to keep you going through even the most menial of chores. Before you look forward, cast your mind back over the last six months and consider those events that came and went; those events that were a long time in planning and will last far longer in the memory. What am I talking about? Well for me it's the weekends away, the holidays, days out in the country, concerts to see my favourite bands, a day at the seaside, a night at the opera, and special meals with even more special people.

We all have a budget of course, and by asking you this question I'm not trying to leave you excited but broke. Think of those things that you are looking forward to with relish that won't leave you scrambling for a payday loan. I'm really looking forward to getting out in the country at the weekend with just my dog for company, side by side for several miles. I say 'just' – there's nothing missing from such an outing, providing the perfect environment and company for me to reflect and make sense of my world while considering what lies ahead. This one man and his dog time for me costs nothing except maybe the price of a car park and the odd poo bag. What are you looking forward to that will cost the same?

Who will that phone call be with? Who will you be playing that sport or hobby alongside or against? What sights, sounds and smells will engage your senses as you hear the noises that you love to hear, see the views that you never tire of capturing and breathe in the aromas that take you to a happy place? While we're on the subject, what are your favourites in each of these sensory categories? I love lists and I've spent many a flight creating my top ten smells, sights and sounds. Over the years it's also made for a great game at family gatherings, guessing who said what to each. Who would have thought that Uncle Mark liked the smell of Johnson's Baby Powder so much!

Create your own 'top tens' then consider how they might cajole you into expanding your 'things I am looking forward to' list. You might be surprised at what pops up. And if you do that little exercise quickly, go back and consider taste and touch for the full house!

Then there's the goals, which for many of us can look like a wish list. 'I'm looking forward to getting fitter' is one I hear alongside 'I'm looking forward to not having to go to work every day'. I'm looking forward to Christmas but there's nothing I can do to bring it forward, unless I am one of those people who decides to erect my tree while everyone else is still applying sun cream. The date is set, same time every year. Yet with regards to getting fitter we do have control, the same as we do for getting richer, getting more sleep, getting more productive, developing more harmonious relationships and the rest.

For these and the ones I haven't mentioned that are relevant for you, look forward to it for sure, but don't sit there expecting things to happen without any involvement from you. What next steps do you need to take to turn the things that you're looking forward to into moments captured forever on your timeline?

I get immense pleasure from looking forward, equalled by the fulfilment I get from looking back and the two are intrinsically linked. So, big and small, look forward to 'em all. Build them into your calendar, plan them, enjoy every moment of them, and know that as you reflect on them once they've happened, no one can ever take the memories away from you.

10. WHAT DO YOU LOVE TO DO THAT YOU GET REWARDED FOR?

I love writing and always have. The silly thing is that for 30 years of my life I lost sight of this, disregarding and discarding it for what I deemed to be more sociable and active pursuits. Why do we often perceive that there is a forced choice when the options can co-exist quite merrily? When I was at primary school the teacher decided that my novels were worthy of being read out in front of the whole class at story time. It wasn't just the writing of the words; it was also playing the role of narrator to an enthralled audience that gave me such an eight-year-old buzz (my age at the time, not its duration). The fact that I didn't start writing again until I was 40 is a real shame, given that it provides me with such satisfaction.

Yet here I am, writing, doing what I love. The fact that I am writing about asking questions and helping people to arrive at their answers is the icing on the cake as that too is something that I love. As a facilitator, helping individuals, teams and organisations get clarity on whatever it is they need to get clarity on is a key part of my role, and I love it!

Love, hey? It's a strong word don't you think, and maybe a word that you can't relate to whatever it is that you get paid to do. So let's separate the one question being posed into two: the first part being 'what do you love to do?' followed by 'what do you get rewarded for?'.

Thirty years flowed under the adolescent bridge and a few more bridges besides before I rekindled my desire to be an author. What have you let slip between then and now that when you stop and cast your mind back, you loved to do? Reflect on what it was that you looked forward to doing, time flew when you were doing it and even though you say it yourself, you were pretty good at doing it as well. I have no idea what you might be thinking about at this point, but ask yourself is it too late to get back in the saddle (regardless of whether you loved horse riding or not)?

We don't have to go all nostalgic on ourselves either. Think about what you love to do at this stage in your life, whatever decade you're firmly ensconced in. It's often the case that we don't start loving something until we've matured somewhat. When I listened to opera as a teenager I thought someone had jumped into an ice cold bath such were the cries of anguish, whereas now it's indulgence and escapism rolled into one.

On a professional note, I never really saw myself as a coach, yet nowadays I get intense satisfaction from reaching successful outcomes in conversations that take place where my goal is to do exactly that. I've warmed to it. What have you grown to love doing in recent times and how do you benefit from doing it? Do you love something because you are good at it or are you good at something because you love it? An interesting conundrum but does it actually matter? It's the fact that they are interwoven that's important.

Now consider what you get rewarded for. I know that reward can come in many guises but just think for a moment about what you get paid to do. Someone has decided that what you do is worth a certain amount. What aspects of that work do you love? For me it is writing, asking questions and coaching – what three spring to mind for you?

If you can't think of anything when faced with that question, you're not alone. Break it down into smaller pieces. For instance, do you enjoy meeting new people, being the face of the company, solving problems, delivering a keynote, taking risks, mending cars, treading the boards or treading the grapes? It would be a dull world if we all loved doing the same things, and it would be a tough world if we all went after the same jobs and subsequently got rewarded for performing the same tasks.

It might be easier for some of us to consider those things that we get rewarded for that we don't love. Now ain't that sad? Yet isn't that life? Who really enjoys doing the ironing or putting the bins out? In my work, form filling is the bane of my life – it drives me nuts! Yet I need to complete some of these less inspiring duties in order to get to a place where the work that I love can materialise. But it should be the minority, and if for you that's not the case, what could you do to shift the balance? What adjustments or changes in direction might you need to make, however big or small, to get rewarded for the things that you love? Don't go handing your notice in just yet though, as maybe those opportunities lie somewhat closer to home. Perhaps you just haven't considered how you might marry the two together yet.

This chapter isn't all about galvanising you to make changes though, it's also about smiling contentedly at the rewards that your endeavours provide you with. People tell me how well behaved my dog is. Well let me tell you, when she arrived at our home at the grand old age of 12 weeks that wasn't quite the case! It took plenty of hard work, hard work that we loved to do and the rewards have been there in bucketloads ever since.

We're not all dog lovers but I bet you can think of your own examples. Just think about how well your kids have turned out, with all their good manners and etiquette (OK so that one might be stretching it a bit!). Think about how hard you've worked to get your home looking the way that it does and the comments people make as they enter in, or how much those spinning classes at the gym that you thrive on have achieved results that you previously thought were unattainable.

Whether we're talking about your dog, your kids, your home, your spinning class, your job or all five, bask in the glory of the rewards that you've achieved as a result of not only the hard work you've put into them, but the love that you have for them.

11. WHERE MIGHT YOU SHOW A LITTLE MORE KINDNESS?

The word kind seems to be making a comeback. After years in the wilderness, replaced in some quarters by an 'every man and woman for himself or herself' mindset, it's now regained its rightful place as one of the go-to qualities. Hallelujah! Let's face it, the world is ready for the kindness renaissance and needs it more than ever right now.

At my last employer, when a new member of our leadership team was introduced my boss made a request to me. She knew that I was unsure of his credentials and that I was seemingly unable to mask my feelings on the matter. "I want you to do something for me – I want you to be kind to him," she said, with grace and clarity. She might not have known it at the time but that simple statement had a great impact on me. For the first time it had me questioning myself on how I showed up in the kindness stakes.

To that point I had never seen myself as anything other than kind, yet as a quality it manifests itself in many ways, some of which were more in line with my approach than others. In that scenario being kind meant being helpful, being respectful and being welcoming – anything that would fast track his ability to hit the ground running and repay the faith shown in him.

Think of the last time that someone new joined your organisation. How would they have perceived the welcome they got from you?

Were you one of those individuals who made them feel at home straight away or rather left them wondering why they ever upped sticks from their previous professional abode? Think about when you last joined a new group of people – a new team, club or circle of friends. Who made you feel like a part of a community where the whole was greater than the sum of its parts, and what actions did they take to do just that?

The request that was made to me was as a result of the individual in question struggling to make the swift impact that both he and the business desired. Within a year he had left our team and left me wondering what I could have done to have ensured that the business got the return on its investment (recruitment is never a cheap exercise), and that the individual saw both me and the company in the most positive light.

On reflection, I know what I could have done. I could have spent more time talking to him, sharing experiences and lessons learned, providing my opinion without being opinionated, answering his questions to fill in the gaps of his knowledge and asking the questions that would have allowed him to reveal some of his own stories, lessons and ideas. I could and should have made him feel a part of something by helping him to understand where his responsibilities dovetailed into everyone else's, finding his place at the table.

Have you ever been in that situation, or are you in a similar one now? It doesn't sit comfortably, the fact that he didn't see the kindest version of me, and I have learned from the experience. Who would benefit from seeing a kinder version of you at the moment and what are some of those small, simple steps that you can take to enable the kindness sunshine to emerge from the clouds?

What's the opposite of being kind, being mean? When faced with that choice it seems pretty obvious really. Being kind is the best option. And if you're still undecided, research at Oxford University suggests that being kind makes you happier, and let's face it, if you had to be one of Snow White's seven dwarves, who wouldn't want to be Happy?

Let's break the people on the receiving end of your kindness down into three separate components, starting with the group that are most important to you – the friends, family and close colleagues who you know well and they know you. Who can you think of in that bunch of fine folk who might benefit from a bit more love and understanding? Before you start saying 'hey, I thought we were talking kindness here?' I would suggest that these are two of the words that you might find in the kindness thesaurus, so don't get picky, it's a big subject!

Who might require more of your time, more of your support, more your empathy? Whether it's a helping hand or a helping ear, which of your nearest and dearest community would benefit from more of you? My work takes me around the world and as a result my diary is full and varied. As all of us do, I strive to achieve balance in my life, juggling the personal and the professional, and on a recent visit to my mother I asked her if there were any jobs that she needed doing. When she told me they had all been completed by other family members, initially I felt slightly hurt and redundant. As all good mothers do, she sensed this and added, "There's no point in asking you to do anything as you're never here."

Good feedback and a good wake-up call. Note to self: be more proactive in offering support and your kind intentions may well progress to actions. Who are you not being kind enough to on the basis that you are just not present enough in that relationship?

What about the middle component – those people that you know but you aren't really that close to? That friend of a friend who shows up on their own at a house party – how welcome do you make them feel? The neighbour who needs a lift to the train station – is that a platform to display your community spirit? The colleague that has to leave early to deal with a minor family crisis – are you on hand to step into their shoes or is that someone else's job?

Finally, what about those people that you've never met – the total strangers? We're talking about those random acts of kindness that we've heard about but maybe never done. Isn't it about time that you dished some of these out? I was once driving on a motorway toll, and unknowingly to me, the driver in front had paid for two to the guy in the pay booth, with me being the welcome recipient of their act. I don't know how they felt having done it but I hope they felt even better than I did having been on the receiving end. Closer to home, my wife has been known to buy a burger for a total stranger in the fast food queue (irrespective of whether they were queuing for a salad or not).

The world is all about give and take, but isn't giving so much more fulfilling? In case you're wondering if you have the budget for such acts, they most definitely do not have to be financial. I was at an airport in the States last week, and on seeing an elderly lady struggle with her suitcase, I carried it up the stairs for her. Now I'm not trying to big myself up here – as far as random acts of kindness go it was pretty small and just basic courtesy – but the look of delight on her face put a spring in my jet-lagged step and I felt good. In fact, I felt happy.

What random acts of kindness might you deliver in the next day or so? Then consider what not so random acts you might demonstrate to those closer to home. I guarantee you'll feel better for having done so. And by the way, whatever you've heard in the past, you don't have to be cruel in the process.

12. WHAT WAS THE LAST THING THAT YOU LEARNED ABOUT YOURSELF?

Seems quite a while since you were at school doesn't it? Those 'best days of your life' spent in the classroom focusing on the three Rs. At my school there were times when it may well have stood for rioting, raging and rebelling, but taking those not so text book attributes aside, it was a time spent learning. We developed, we grew, and when the dust settled, we learned.

Of course the famed reading, writing and arithmetic were all high on the list but there was much more learning that took place than merely what was on the curriculum for that year. We learned about ourselves, and others, as we began the ongoing journey of increasing self-awareness. We made mistakes, we got into scrapes, were punished, penalised, corrected and nurtured. And putting that eclectic mix together, ultimately we grew, forming the person that we are today.

So what's happened since those days have passed? Are you a life-long learner or did you leave all that behind when the final school bell tolled? Let's hope for your sake that you didn't because in reality we never stop learning about life and those people who populate it, not least ourselves.

If you're like me you probably bury your head in books, surf the internet and watch quiz shows on the television all in the thirst for knowledge. You may know that the capital of Ecuador isn't the letter E in your trivial pursuit of pot luck answers, and you no doubt earn a small fortune every time you answer questions on your sofa when you watch re-runs of *Who Wants to Be a Millionaire?* But let's put the pub quiz superhero in us all to one side and consider what was the last thing that you learned about yourself. Where have you surprised, challenged or frustrated yourself, and in doing so revealed a part of you that you were previously unaware of?

I spend a lot of time operating as a single traveller, checking in and out of hotels with great regularity, with a passport used as often as most people's front door keys. It's a lifestyle I'm used to, but on a recent trip I found myself feeling lower than normal. As I reflected on why this might be I considered how much time I had recently spent in my own company. It dawned on me how the words alone and lonely are seemingly quite different, yet for me they were intrinsically linked. It was obvious when I thought about it, but to that point I hadn't.

What situation do you find yourself in frequently and what impact does it have on you? I learned that I need to limit the amount of time I spend alone to avoid feeling lower than I want to feel and have taken action to ensure that this is the case. What could you learn from the situations you find yourself in and what actions might emerge as a result?

Recently I was delivering a workshop that took behavioural training to a deeper level. It was pretty intensive stuff I can tell you and I was relishing the chance to take people on a journey of exploration. Being as professional and polished as I could be, imagine my irritation then when my co-facilitator said to me, "Mike, this is important stuff and you are trying to be too funny. There's a time and a place." This was news to me as I couldn't have been more serious if I had tried, yet all feedback is good feedback and all that. I learned that even when I am being as strait-laced as

I can be, my approach can come across as a bit slapstick to some, which might in turn get in the way of the key messages that I am trying to put across.

What recent feedback have you received that you initially wanted to reject but ended up taking on the chin? What did you learn about yourself as a result?

As for the last thing that I learned about myself, I need look no further than a recent domestic conversation that's still hot off the press. Since running my own company it's fair to say that my main focus has been on doing just that. I've been less inclined to play an active part in ensuring that 'project home' runs smoothly. I don't mean the relationships, I mean the ongoing management of the house – the duties and the DIY that need to be seen to, otherwise, before you know it, things go rapidly downhill. Over the last couple of weeks there have been several scenarios where my lack of knowledge combined with an even greater lack of desire have resulted in the responsibility for all these tasks sitting with one person. Guess what? It wasn't me.

The issue is that I have become blissfully unaware of how many things actually work. There have been many changes in our home in the last four years: we have a new boiler, a new alarm, a new washing machine, a new this and an even newer that. None of which, once you get past the basics, do I have a clue how to operate. Even my smartphone with its regular software updates flummoxes me. The one person who is able to make all of them work said the other day, in her own wonderful way, "I worry every day what you would do if anything ever happened to me." This was no gentle rebuke; this was an honest assessment of the current situation and a concern on how I would function on a daily basis. She didn't say it, but I heard it – I'm useless when it comes to this type of stuff. Add the finances into the mix, which I have no involvement in whatsoever, and without her I am well and truly stuffed. Time for me to pull my finger and the manuals out.

Think of the feedback that you've received, the situations you've been in and the conversations you've taken part in. What was the last thing that you actually learned about yourself, and what are you going to do about it?

Right then, I best get back to work – these bills don't pay themselves you know, or so I've just learned.

13. WHO DO YOU NEED TO FORGIVE?

When you stop and think about how many people have come and gone in your life you probably end up with a cast of thousands. Consider all those people that you've had a relationship with, sometimes successfully and other times less so.

Let's think about those who fit into the 'gone' category for a moment. People leave us for many reasons and quite simply one of those reasons is that there is often no longer a need to keep in touch. On other occasions people may change jobs or locations, and despite there being an initial desire to remain forever friends, the strength of connection isn't enough to ensure that out of sight doesn't mean out of mind. Then there is another bunch, hopefully somewhat smaller, who we fell out with, and as a result one of the parties decided to untie whatever kind of knot existed.

As you reflect on who might form a part of that select band of not so merry men and women, are there any of them that still occupy your thoughts and have you reaching for your voodoo doll? Before you start justifying your thoughts, feelings and emotions on every person that you've ever made an enemy out of, I'm not suggesting that you wipe the slate clean here giving each and every character who has ever had the temerity to cross you a fresh start. My job is merely to ask the question, the task I set you is to give thought to your answer and then see if any actions might spill out of that answer. Phew, I wouldn't want to get on the wrong side of you!

So who do you need to forgive? I'm also not suggesting that you have to dig out the phone book and make call after call, building bridges over every river that ever flowed around you. But just consider those negative emotions that fester within; where might you be better off letting some of them head out to sea, creating space for something altogether more uplifting and positive?

I go on an annual walking weekend with a group of guys who worked together in the 90s. It's been taking place now for over 20 years and what started off as a gang of four soon grew to 14, with various individuals requesting an invitation before being accepted to join the motley crew. It's been several years now since the number increased further, but earlier this year a request came in from Simon, a good friend of mine. Having viewed the pictures from previous years on social media, he thought it provided a great opportunity to get in touch with some of his old colleagues, some of whom he considered to be friends, while getting some exercise and fresh air in the bargain.

The request initially came to me, and I subsequently passed it to the 'founding committee' of the annual walk, who thought it appropriate to put it to the vote. The majority vote, however, wouldn't win. It was decided that if there was one single vote against the newbie then he wouldn't come – simple as that. The good news for Simon was that 13 people said yes. The bad news was that one said no. He still doesn't know who declined his request, and I hope that if he did then he would forgive him, which is more than can be said for the owner of the black ball!

Over a beer at the weekend that ensued, we joked about who we thought had voted against his inclusion, and having taken it in turns to give a few plausible (and a few more less plausible) guesses, one of the founding committee revealed that it was he who decided that the number of walkers would grow no more. The reason: Simon had turned his partner down for a job over 25 years ago.

Revenge, they say, is a dish best served cold, and on this occasion it was practically freezing. He had not forgiven him for something that happened three decades ago despite his life being nothing other than a great success story ever since.

I was shocked but it really got me thinking, and now writing, about this subject. Take a journey back in time and consider who you would do that to, and whether it would help even things up or just reveal a side of you that isn't actually that beneficial to you or those around you. What do you need to let go of? Memories are so much more pleasant when they are populated with positive times, productive conversations, and people whom you recall with fondness. Do you really need to clutter your memory bank with negative stuff? What would the benefit be to you if you were to forgive? Would any of those relationships help you now should you decide to bury the hatchet rather than use it in anger? If so, which ones and how? What should you do and when?

I fell out with a friend of mine many years ago. We had two great years together, thick as thieves, frequenting bars, travelling the country to see our team play and watching our favourite bands perform live. It was a silly fall-out really, just two stubborn guys thinking they were right and as a result choosing not to speak. Six months on, I changed jobs and location and the relationship stopped. Six months further and I met a mutual colleague in the street who said, "Such a shame about Mark wasn't it?" Unbeknown to me he had been diagnosed with leukaemia shortly after the last time I saw him, and within the space of a few weeks had died. We were both 20. We fell out over a beer-fuelled conversation about a girl who I had fancied. He was a good lad was Mark, and I wish that I had forgiven him, and vice versa. My memories of the good times are as clear as ever, and the decision I made not to forgive him denied me of a precious few more in the short time that he had left.

It might not be life and death in every situation but who do you need to forgive before it's too late?

14. WHAT SHOULD YOU BE READING MORE OF?

Mark Twain had it right when he said, "The man who doesn't read has no advantage over the man that can't." Having got this far I know that you belong to neither category and I reckon that's a cause for us both to celebrate. Why are you reading this? That's not an invitation for you to stop by the way but a chance to reflect on your rationale for picking up a book in the first place, or a magazine, or a newspaper. Hopefully I have an idea of some of the reasons why you're reading the words I'm currently writing, so let's focus on reading in general. Is it to relax, to escape or for enjoyment purposes? It's likely to be one or more of them if we're talking about burying your head in a good novel.

But let me reassure you, everything that you're reading within these pages are my questions, my thoughts and my ideas, populated with my experiences, and most definitely no fairytale. I still want you to enjoy it and to escape into a world of self-reflection, but I want you to read it for more than that. I want you to feel more ready, willing and able to make changes. I want to galvanise you into some form of personal development.

If you consider the last newspaper that you picked up, it was probably for a different set of reasons. What pages did you dive straight into – the front page headlines, the gossip column, what's on TV or, like me, did you head round the back to catch up on all the latest sports news? That might depend on whether your newspaper of choice is broadsheet or tabloid, whether your requirement was to be informed or entertained, and whether you were more interested in the words or pictures.

Regardless of whether the last thing you read consisted of glossy pages or was in a tablet format, our reasons for reading are wide and varied. Yet what we do know is that reading increases our vocabulary, it stimulates our mind, it helps us learn and it reduces our levels of stress. It also makes us better writers, but keep off the shelves for a while will you, I'd like to sell a few more copies of this first without adding to the competition!

Now I don't want to stop your literary fun, so the question here isn't what should you be reading less of but rather what is missing from your library? What have you never read that you would benefit from reading? What would challenge your current thinking?

I'm not getting on a political, spiritual or moral high-horse here but it's not too controversial a comment to make when I say that the world has never been so connected yet simultaneously we are so distant from one another. It's scary and in many cases it's ignorant. We all have a view but how often is this view formed with only certain pieces of the jigsaw to hand?

I visited a good friend recently and was surprised, maybe shocked, to see a copy of the Quran on their sideboard, but it all made perfect sense when they explained the reason why it was there. "All I know about Islam is what I hear on the television and see in the newspapers," she said. "I want to get a deeper understanding of the beliefs and ideology that lie behind the faith." In order to reach an informed opinion, you need to be informed. That was their view, quite different from the 'join the dots' approach taken by so many so often. What content are you missing that, if you had it, would enable you to be more informed in your thinking, judgment and decision making? Where would you find that content and what should you be reading more of in your quest?

The urban myth in these shores is that you are never more than six feet away from a rat. I'm not too sure about that one so it's probably far truer to say that, as I write in 2019, you are never more than six minutes away from a Brexit-related discussion. The television is awash with rich insight into the pros and cons of going it alone. Such a shame then that the same wasn't the case when the vote was actually made, with so many people casting their vote with such limited information and having not done their homework.

If you are reading in the UK and you voted, think of what you know about the whole debate that you didn't know when you placed your cross in the ballot box. We are closer now to the complete picture, the whole story, and with greater understanding comes a greater ability to take part in constructive discussion. What discussions have you missed out on due to a lack of knowledge on the subject in question? Any desire to do anything about it so you don't just sit there playing the involuntary role of the silent minority?

Putting politics and religion to one side, let me take you to an altogether more relaxing and rejuvenating place – your last summer holiday. What books accompanied you on your jaunt, if any, and which of them provided you with most pleasure? Which books were you reading when you lost all track of time, leading to your travelling companion wondering if they should just take themselves off on their own day trip such was the lack of conversation emanating from your lips?!

You're back home now though, so why confine such pleasures to the sunbed? Think of the sheer escapism that those precious few hours afforded you and consider where they can be replicated in less hedonistic surroundings. After all, we each need to lose ourselves once in a while. My favourite bookshelf in our office is simple – it's the shelf that houses all those books that are patiently waiting to be read. It's a combination of purchases I've made from my favourite authors, recommendations from friends and the occasional wild card that drew me in with an interesting title or a captivating paragraph on the back cover.

What's on your unread bookshelf? Oh no, I bet you haven't got one have you? I can read you like a book.

15. WHO NEEDS YOUR ADVICE AND WHEN SHOULD YOU BE GIVING IT?

The hardest thing about being a parent of adult 'children' in my experience is the letting go. When they were too young to know any better I could spray my opinion, demands, commands and advice like confetti with the majority of it (like at a wedding) landing on the floor rather than the intended 'target'. Fast forward 20 plus years in my case and life is a bit different. When my eldest daughter informed me that she was going to get her biggest tattoo yet, and by virtue of the fact the most expensive, it had me yearning to regain my role of chief rebuker, ready to provide punitive feedback regardless of whether it was sought or not.

Yet I believe that this is no longer my role. If she chooses to locate some skin that is currently free from ink and replace it with something that she would describe as art, what does my opinion matter, unless of course she asks for it?

That's the difference now that my three girls are in their mid-20s. They come to me for advice when they want it and when they recognise that they would benefit from it. It's worth noting at this point that they don't come to me for advice on how to build the latest DIY chest of drawers or how to get their car firing on all cylinders again, because they know me well enough to know that I would be as much use as an ashtray on a motorbike in such instances.

They do come to me, however, for my thoughts on how to deal with their latest relationship challenge or how to resolve conflict in their workplace. They ask me to share my experiences on the places that I've explored on my travels as they plot their next adventure, and they disclose their thoughts, feelings and emotions to me, anticipating more than a sympathetic ear in response. They do this because they think that I can help them move forward in whatever situation in these areas they feel stuck in, and I agree with them.

What advice could you be giving if someone were to ask you for it and who would that someone be? In the *Mastermind* of life what would your chosen specialist subject be, and while I'm on the subject of TV quizzes, who would have you at the top of their list for 'phone a friend'?

You may or may not agree with my approach to the parenting game. I know for sure that my own mother doesn't, swift as she is to give advice on anything and everything in the expectation that it will lead to a change of behaviour or immediate action. In 2001 I made the decision to shave all my hair off. To put that sentence into some context, it was my hair that made the majority of that decision, I just decided to put the ever diminishing amount that remained out of its misery. My mother's reaction was unsurprising when she said, "Well how ridiculous, who is going to want to work with you looking like that?" It's your choice as a parent I guess, how and when you give advice, and it's your choice as a friend, neighbour, colleague or boss how and when you give it too.

So who might actually benefit from some of your advice even though they haven't been knocking at your door to get your perspective? When have you benefited from someone doing just that? What advice would that be? From your angle, where and how can you see a situation, a chain of events differently and by imparting that insight to another how would it enable them to view a more complete picture?

As you look back on your career what are those pearls of wisdom that people have imparted to you? They may have been said as a throwaway comment but they stuck with you, and the words remained with you ready to be put to use as and when required. One of my favourite bosses, George, a blunt Yorkshireman once shared something with me and he will have no idea how often I refer to it.

He was the director of a training company that I was previously employed by and he had recently recruited a new Head of Sales. I had observed George in various meetings asking this guy what his opinion was on a particular subject, and more often than not the response was akin to 'yes I agree with you George, I think you're right'. He didn't last long in the role, and shortly after, George invited me to lunch to get my fresh thoughts on the business. This provided me with an opportunity to ask him some questions so I asked him why the new Head of Sales came and went in the space of six weeks.

"Simple," he said. "He didn't have an opinion. My advice for you, Mike, as you go up the ladder in your career: always have an opinion. The skill is to know when to share it." George would smile if he knew that I was writing about this, a generation later. It wouldn't be a beaming smile, that wasn't his way, but he'd smile in his own characteristically dour manner.

Someone somewhere views you in the same way that I viewed George – as a person whose opinion and advice are worth listening to. Advice that would hold them in good stead, not only for the future but the present. Whose George are you, and what would they benefit from hearing? The skill, as my main man said, is to know when the time is right to provide your thoughts.

Ask yourself these questions before you open your mouth. Is your advice going to be given with positive intent? Does the recipient have a choice what to do with the advice? Is it relevant? Will it benefit the recipient to hear your thoughts? If the answer to all of these questions is yes, then I suggest that the time might be right for you to share.

I once worked with a young guy who, poor lad, had a terrible problem with body odour. People used to talk about him behind his back, yet no one was willing to give him some feedback that might shed light on why all of his colleagues appeared reticent to venture into the small room where he worked, surrounded by the printers that were his domain. One of my colleagues decided that he needed to act, and in what I thought was a brave move, gave him some candid feedback and a can of advice disguised as deodorant. Some may see that as bold and others may see it as brutal, but as I consider the four questions that I gave you, it passed all four checks. There was a positive intent, he had a choice whether to take the advice on board, it was relevant, and the individual benefited. The difference was so tangible you could smell it.

He took the advice that he was given on board – will you?

16. WHERE COULD YOU LISTEN MORE EFFECTIVELY AND HOW?

'You've got two ears and one mouth' was something that I was regularly reminded of in my younger days. It's probably been said in more recent times too, but I might not have been listening. The old adage that suggests that we should spend more time listening than talking probably provides food for thought for all of us but the reality is, of course, that some people are worth listening to more than others.

At a high level we can categorise the reasons for listening into three separate areas. Firstly, you are seeking to receive information and knowledge that will be useful to you. Secondly, you are interested in the other person and what they have to say as you seek to cement or further develop your relationship with them. And finally, it's common courtesy to listen to someone when they are speaking to you.

Let's focus on that first category for now. Who currently has information that you would benefit from receiving and who has knowledge on a subject that you would either like or need to understand more about? Knowing who these people are is the first and biggest step to setting about acquiring that stuff that you're looking for. This is a big area. If I left you alone for a while you would potentially end up with a list longer than this chapter of names of people who know more than you do about topics that you would benefit from knowing more about.

The second step is behaving in a style that encourages the other person to share their knowledge with you. In other words, be a good listener. When I received my first ever personality profiling assessment many moons ago it told me that I was likely to be perceived as a poor listener. In amongst an array of statements that I felt hit the nail on the head this was one that I rejected. However, on witnessing my chagrin, a colleague and friend (same person) provided me with feedback that has stuck with me for over 20 years. If feedback is the breakfast of champions, I didn't have to eat a further thing all day such was its size, and it came in three distinct courses.

"When I am talking to you, you are always doing something else," he shared. "Or when I am in mid-sentence you interrupt me, and that gives me the impression that you aren't interested in what I have to say." He didn't stop there, and added a third component to the trilogy by stating, "When you do wait for me to finish what I have to say, you then start talking about a completely different subject."

OK then, so maybe the profile was right and I had some work to do in this area. Do you? Are you guilty of any of these three listening crimes, or is there a different set of charges that can be levelled at you? In order to spend more time listening to others, what might you need to do differently in order to reap the benefits of having an audience with them?

Now consider the second category that I referred to – those people who you are interested in. Listening is an attractive attribute. People like to feel as though they have been heard, so if you want to develop an even more effective relationship with someone, demonstrate that you are listening to them. Who would consider you to be even more of a special friend, confidante or a part of their inner circle if you were to listen more to what they have to say? Think of those relationships that have suffered over the years, that aren't quite as strong as they used to be. How would these people describe your listening capabilities?

There's a difference between hearing what someone has said and demonstrating that you have listened. In *The Seven Habits of Highly Effective People* Dr Stephen Covey identified five levels of listening. He started off with 'ignoring' – where no effort is made. Not the best strategy I would suggest if you are seeking to win friends and influence people. He moved on to 'pretending', something we've probably all been guilty of, as is 'selective', the third of the five levels, where we switch on and off depending on the subject being spoken about. Crikey, three of five levels covered and we're still nowhere near achieving 'good listener' status!

The fourth level moves us to something a bit more positive – 'attentive' listening where finally we are actually listening to what is being said in such a manner that we would be able to replay it back if called on to do so.

But in order to be the 'highly effective' person that Covey alluded to we need to progress to the fifth of the five levels. What is that? you may ask. Well if you listen, I'll tell you. 'Empathic' listening is when we listen with both the head and the heart, not only to what is being said but also what isn't being said, to understand the speaker's words, intent and feelings. When was the last time that you can say with certainty and clarity that this intricate statement described you?

When do you need to listen more to your heart and when might you benefit from listening more to your head? When asked about his thoughts on leadership, Nelson Mandela proclaimed, "A good head and a good heart are always a formidable combination." But

I hear you say, we're talking about listening not about leadership. I would suggest the two are inextricably linked. Develop your listening prowess and you will become a better leader, starting with leading yourself.

We had a new TV delivered and fitted recently and it came with an array of weird buttons, features and benefits. The manual was as big as the screen and we were grateful for the support of the guy from the shop when he offered to install it and train us how to use it at no extra cost! We listened intently to what he had to say. We didn't listen empathically, as that would have been a bit silly, but listen we did so we got the benefit from our shiny new entertainment system. So empathic listening might be the answer in certain situations, but as this scenario shows, it doesn't always have to be.

We need to select what we listen to, why we listen to it and how we listen to it. And so do you. And the best way to demonstrate that you're listening – ask an open question. Need any help? Damn, that's a closed one, but you get my drift.

17. WHAT FEARS DO YOU NEED TO CHALLENGE OR CONFRONT?

I've had a pretty traumatic morning I can tell you, taken hostage in my own home by a frog! It was all going so well as I neared the end of the first dog walk of the day, but then as I approached my front door with key in hand I saw it, staring at me with its teeth bared on the doorstep, frothing at the mouth as it blocked my path to safety. If you're not scared of frogs then you're probably wondering what on earth I am going on about, creating a lot of amphibian fuss about nothing. I don't blame you – I'd probably do the same if you revealed to me some of your own irrational fears.

We all have them for whatever reason – ridiculous to some and incomprehensible to others but we all have them. Consider your childhood for a moment and remind yourself of all those fears that you had way back then. As I cast my mind back to some of my first memories there were two types of men (and they always were men in the 70s) who occupied my darkest thoughts the most: dustbin men and clowns. Tuesday was my worst day of the week because that was the day when they would venture into our cul-de-sac. Not the clowns, they had to wait until their yearly visit to my home town, but the refuse collectors. I was just certain that when no one was looking they would throw me into their monstrous contraption, reducing me to the size of one of their grubby hands and no one would hear my screams. The distant sound of them entering the street mob-handed in their truck would render me a quivering wreck and I would flee to the most remote part of our home where I could be sure that they couldn't see me.

The clowns were an altogether more sinister bunch. How anyone could derive enjoyment from this band of merry men was beyond me. At this tender age my mind would go into overdrive, wondering what lay beneath the make-up. In my dramatic world they were the most evil of evil characters, making the dustbin men look saintly by comparison. Half a century later and my fears of both have dissipated and I reckon that I probably owe an apology to both, realising now that they were merely trying to make a living.

What perceptions do you need to challenge from both then and now? What fears do you have that you recognise have been blown out of all proportion? As I look at the situation objectively, the frog, small enough to place on the palm of my hand, can do me no harm. If you were to look at your fear objectively what would you be saying?

As a point of clarity, this chapter is in no way seeking to replace any professional help that you might require. Many of us are left contorted by phobias that are way beyond my realm of expertise. Whether it be open or confined spaces, spiders or heights, the world is full of experiences that may or may not happen that leave us in a state of hideous panic. But what fears could or should you be confronting? What could you do that might dispel the worst thoughts that you have on a subject?

Within the space of three years I went from being petrified of clowns to volunteering to be a part of their act – front row, arm outstretched waiting to be picked, cheeky smile – so what happened to make the transition? In my juvenile head I just decided one day that it looked a bit childish to be fearful of something that was meant to be a bit of fun so I needed to face my fear head on.

Being a part of their act would either accentuate the issue or make it better and it was a gamble that I was prepared to take. I took the plunge and that's one way I guess. What fear should you be confronting by jumping head first straight in?

That's not always going to work though, so another route that takes things a bit more gradually is known in fear circles as 'exposure'. I'm not sure if there is such a circle in existence, but for the sake of this topic let's assume that there is. If you were scared of the dark as a child look back on how you made the transition from light on to light off. The chances are that the light went gradually darker rather than the flick of a switch one weekend. The amount of time that you slept (or stayed awake) in the pitch black increased over a period of time. Gradual exposure helps us make the change. What small steps could you take that would 'expose' you to your fears?

Consider your biggest fear and write down all the scenarios and issues that you can imagine that you are afraid of. Then rank them from smallest to biggest – eat the elephant one slice at a time as they say, with apologies to vegetarians and those who have a fear of our planet's largest land mammal. I'm not ready to hold a frog just yet but I am ready to stand close to one and watch it hop around. The latter is more attainable to me than the former.

As you rank the list you are creating what is known as your own 'fear ladder', preparing yourself to take steps up the ladder to confront your fear, and if you're afraid of climbing ladders then you're making real progress at this early stage! As you consider your fear, what are the smallest fears that are related to it that you could address, and in doing so start your ascent up the ladder?

In his inaugural address President Roosevelt famously said, "We have nothing to fear but fear itself." As you reflect on his words, what do they mean to you? What fears should you be challenging? One definition of fear is that it is 'an emotional reaction to imminent danger'. With that in mind, in many situations it is a very real and very understandable emotion, yet the frog probably never caused me imminent danger. I've just looked out of the window and he or she (its gender remains a mystery to me) has disappeared to a safer haven. I need to take some steps up this particular fear ladder just as I did with the clowns. As for the bin men, it's Monday today so they can wait one more day.

18. WHAT GIFT WOULD YOU BENEFIT FROM RECEIVING RIGHT NOW?

It's early January as I type and our home has just returned to its familiar look, with the decorations, lights and assortment of festive regalia sent back up to the attic where they reside for 11 months of the year. It was a hectic period for us with eight people (and two dogs) of three generations waking up in our home on Christmas morning, taking it in turns to rip off the wrapping paper on presents of various shapes and sizes.

We've always been a family where gifts are exchanged at this time of year – the thoughtful, the sought after, the funny and the surprising – they all form part of the deluge of giving and receiving, where maybe the emphasis has been more on quantity than quality at times!

That's not meant to sound ungrateful but it's fair to say that some of the gifts that I received will see the light of day more than others. I'm sitting here in my new socks underneath a new pair of trainers and I smell of a new aftershave. All three have quickly integrated themselves into my world, yet others have swiftly found themselves relegated to the drawer under my side of the bed where they became acquainted with some of their previous year's counterparts!

Prior to the season of goodwill, I am asked by loved ones to create a list so that they can go in search of something that I've told them to go in search of, and invariably I scratch my head as I consider what I would benefit from receiving that would constitute a successful gift. What was on your list this year, regardless of whether it was passed on to others or not? What did you want or need this year more than any other? I hope you got it, and if you did how is it being put to good use? Don't tell me it's under your bed.

On this occasion though, it's only me who is asking you, so the pressure is off. So go on then, what gift would you benefit from receiving right now? What would make your life easier, more enjoyable, more comfortable or more exciting? Look back at that last sentence – which of those four is most important to you? If you received a pair of furry slippers it might add to your comfort levels but probably not impact your excitement scale too much, and that might suit you just fine.

A friend once told me that the definition of a great present is something that when you open it, you're delighted to receive it but you wouldn't have bought it for yourself. I got a gorgeous pair of cufflinks for my 50th birthday. Thinking about it, I can't remember ever buying myself any cufflinks yet they've always been a welcome gift, put to use within a couple of weeks. I once received a football signed by players of my favourite team. That's something I'd never think of going to the trouble of acquiring myself, but it was gleefully received. What would your ball and cufflinks be?

Let's change focus though and think of those gifts where money doesn't have to be exchanged and receipts don't need to be kept. What, if someone were to give it to you, would be received with pleasure, gratitude and no little relief? Apparently the best things in life are free, so what would you love to receive that wouldn't cost a penny?

Does this list come to you any easier than the one that you get asked to provide at various times of the year when celebrations are the order of the day? Let me try and help you get off the mark. What would you like to see? Where would you like to go? Who would you like to meet? What would you like to hear? What would you like someone to take off your hands? What would save you time? What would help you relax? What would help you become better at what you do? The answer to all those questions won't have to result in money being thrown at a situation.

Now allow yourself to dream a little. I'd love to receive the gift of sleep. It's amazing how many gifts I've received over the years from loved ones on this subject. From pillow sprays to bath salts, relaxation CDs to eye masks, and you won't find one of them under my bed I can tell you – all put to use in my quest for some shut eye. In all honesty however, they've not worked and I'd love to be able to put my head on the pillow at 10pm, waking the following day at 7am just once. What an incredible gift that would be!

What gift would change your life for the better that can't be wrapped up?

I'm conscious that as I write this chapter it might feel that there is no particular call to action and it's not my style to galvanise you to merely create a wish list that goes nowhere or to no one, so let me try and address that. As you reflect on those things that you want, that you really, really want (Spice Girls albums included), what could you do that would get you closer to being the actual recipient of them?

Is there a conversation that you should be having, a decision you should be making or a question you should be asking that will take you closer to your gift of choice?

The title question asks you what gift would you benefit from receiving. How about getting clarity on the benefit? A gift only gets put to good use if you can see the benefit of taking it out of the actual or metaphorical box. As you consider the gift that you most want to receive, how will your lot improve as a result of receiving it? What will you be able to do once received that you couldn't do without the gift?

The reality is that we are all constantly receiving gifts from others, they just don't come wrapped in a bow. Are you aware, are you grateful and are you reciprocating? What gift did you receive yesterday and what will you receive today? Or right now for that matter? There's no time like the present.

19. WHERE IS YOUR HAPPY PLACE AND ARE YOU SPENDING ENOUGH TIME THERE?

I'm in Boscastle, Cornwall at the moment, typing away in the middle of winter in a snug cottage by the sea. The fire is on and my dog is sleeping by my side. That's not me trying to sound smug, or suggesting that my life is complete, although I do actually like it rather a lot. My intention behind this opening burst of perceived perfection will hopefully soon become apparent so bear with me if you will.

For those for whom geography is not their strong point, or those who hail from other lands, Cornwall is in the far south-west of England surrounded by 300 miles of sea and only connected to the rest of the country by Devon. Unless you can swim rather well there is nowhere else to go once you get here. In the summer millions of families come here for some peace and quiet, blissfully unaware of either the irony or that the crowded beaches that they frequent once they've arrived are empty in January. Don't you go telling them that though as we quite enjoy having the place to ourselves!

It's the perfect place for me to walk, think, relax and enjoy the good food and company on offer. And on this occasion it's also providing the perfect environment for my words to flow and my book to grow.

In short, Cornwall is my happy place. I've never had a bad experience here. Within moments of arriving I'm in a good place, literally and proverbially. When I'm feeling frantic, unproductive or out of control I hear Cornwall calling. When I think of Cornwall, knowing that it is attainable and not just a dream, I always feel that bit better. Just writing about it has put a contented smile on my face. Where is your happy place? What words spring to mind as you reflect on the time that you've spent there and how often are you able to top up your tank by paying it a visit?

In order to get to this happy place of mine we need to load the car and travel for five hours. The challenge with this of course is that if I am in need of a quick fix it's not just around the corner. So maybe we need not just one happy place but a whole plethora of them so you're never too far away from one or more of them, engulfed by a network of happy places.

They don't have to break the bank either or require you to get behind a wheel for 300 miles. Think of that park that you like to frequent, that resting point where the view provides you with much needed reflection time, that comfy corner where you can slip into temporary anonymity, or that cave of yours where you become king or queen of your castle however briefly it might seem. What about that preferred spot in your favourite café, the jacuzzi at the local health club, or, if you're like me, right in the middle of the boisterous crowd at the ball game!

We all have them, and what's more, we all need them. My chosen cross-trainer at the gym does exactly what it aims to do by putting a spring in my step. The seat that has been mine at the home ground of my favourite football team for over 25 years gives me 90 minutes of escapism every two weeks from the hectic world that I am surrounded by. The bench perfectly positioned overlooking the water at one of the parks where we walk our dog is ideal for appreciating what I have on my doorstep, using my senses to breathe in the sights, sounds and smells around me. That's a pretty eclectic mix that I've created all within touching distance, provided you have very, very long arms. What would your list consist of – those happy places that are in reach should you want or need to retreat to them? Where are you sitting, standing or kneeling and who might be by your side?

If you're having a spot of bother identifying where these places are it may just be that you haven't used the term 'happy place' before. Don't let it put you off – I don't want you to think that every time you pay it a visit you automatically become happier about everything and anything as though a switch has been flicked. I wear socks that are designed by the colourful brand Happy Socks. I really like them and they make a vibrant addition to my sock drawer but I've not noticed any difference to my happiness levels to date when wearing them in preference to my other less happy socks.

Yet anything that can nudge you, however slightly, incrementally towards being in a 'better place' can only be good for you and those around you. So if you're not enamoured by calling it a happy place, what word do you prefer – relaxing, recharging, favourite place? Or how about 'home'?

When I return to Cornwall with my wife, there is a song by Ed Sheeran that we play at the same time on our journey. We have our timing down to perfection after so many visits, and as we turn the corner that finally permits us to see the idyllic and atmospheric fishing village nestled below, where land meets the wide expanse of sea, the lyrics 'should this be the last thing I see, I want you to know it's enough for me' are sung by Ed, Mike and Marisa in perfect emotional harmony. It feels like we've come home.

Apart from home, where feels like home for you? Where does it feel like you can just be yourself, surrounded by familiarity? And hey, if your final answer on this subject is 'home', your happy place is home and the place that feels like home is home, then that's great. Who am I to say that any answer you give to this or any other question in this book is unsatisfactory? But there's a big world out there, down there, over there. There's a happy world to explore, full of nooks and crannies waiting for you to call your happy place. Places that will have you singing song lyrics that have special meaning to you as you edge closer to them. Places that will knock your socks off, regardless of whether they were happy ones or not.

20. WHAT SHOULD YOU STOP GIVING YOURSELF A HARD TIME OVER?

We're none of us perfect are we? You might think that some people are well on their way and there are some who might think that they themselves come pretty close, but in reality neither you nor they score the perfect ten in the gymnastics display of life. There's nothing wrong with setting the bar high, and I'm all for stretching to achieve seemingly unattainable goals in the pursuit of being the best that you can be, but this self-flagellation has got to stop!

If you're anything like me, the person that you are in most conversation with is yourself, that inner voice judging you for what you have and haven't done or what you should or shouldn't be doing. The one that proves that hindsight really is a wonderful thing. How much of your own inner voice is constructive, reassuring or galvanising, making a productive contribution to your decision making or adding to your feelings of self-worth?

Compare that to the percentage of time spent when it is eating away at how you feel about the contribution that you make to your family, your place of employment and society at large. Or when it is criticising what you have said or done, calling you names that you wouldn't dream of calling others. Yes, you know the ones – say them now, out loud if you really wish, then write them down on a piece of paper, screw it up then throw it in the waste paper bin, because that's what they are – waste. Pure garbage.

Of course, there are times when a swift internal rebuke is needed. Literally giving yourself a kick up the backside may well be nigh on impossible unless you're one of those gymnasts that I mentioned earlier, but sometimes the figure of speech version is useful to ensure that you don't slack. Really though, is there any need to continuously shower yourself with words ending in 'less'? Clueless, thoughtless, worthless, tactless? Less of it.

What are the recurring themes that form the basis of this negative self-talk? My bet is that it will be a pick and mix of a number of topics ranging from aspects of what you look like, what you have said, how you behave, how you reacted and responded to a situation, and how you have spent your time and money. Did I win my bet? It was odds on really as when it comes to that internal chit chat we're all the same. We could all pick at least one from every one of those pots. Which one is particularly current for you at the moment? Which one is constant, pecking away at you like the enemy within, refusing to appreciate all your successes, much preferring to highlight the occasional misdemeanour?

You look great. And, if you really wanted to do something about how you look, the chances are that you could. I'm completely bald and I often wonder what it would be like to look smooth and suave with a classy hair do. If I really wanted to I could pay for treatment, but hey, bald can be beautiful too. Stop giving yourself a hard time, Mike. And that excess you put on in December, it'll go, it always does.

Thirty years ago I wanted to deliver presentations to large groups but realised that my voice wouldn't allow me to perform such a public task. I couldn't roll my Rs and say my THs properly, and as the old joke goes, 'you can't say fairer than that'. Three decades later, I recognise that I needn't have given myself such a hard time, and 3,000 public presentations later there hasn't been one situation where someone said 'he seemed like a nice bloke but I couldn't understand a word he was saying'.

So much that we give ourselves a hard time over is observed and experienced differently by those around us, and not just those that care for us. When are you your fiercest critic, and how does it help and hinder you? If the former is more powerful than the latter, then go for it; if not, then challenge it.

We all have those 'me and my big mouth' moments or have occasionally pressed send too quickly when reacting rather than responding to an email that irked us, but it's gone. Lay off the self-abuse. Apologise if you think it's appropriate, replace the verbal or written words with a more considered alternative if it truly reflects your thoughts and feelings, but move on – they have.

The chances are that at some point you've been late for a family occasion or missed a friend's birthday. You forgot to call when you said you would or that errand that you promised to do slipped your mind because you were too preoccupied with something else. Well aren't you just pure evil? Or how about par for the course? Your brain, like everyone else's, can only hold so many snippets of information at any one time. Sometimes we forget, and if it wasn't that it might have been something even more important.

Learn from the experience and consider what you might do to prevent such memory lapses from reoccurring, then remove the sack cloth and venture out in public with your head held high! Giving yourself hell isn't going to help anyone, least of all yourself. So what do you need to stop giving yourself a hard time over?

As for how you spend your money, we all have a choice how we spend it, whether we are down to our last 50 pence or £50 million. You had a choice and you chose to buy that new outfit or splash out on that expensive bottle of wine. Some call it extravagance and some call it impulse. How about calling it a choice and one that you may or may not choose to make again. It's gone so let it go. Blame looks backwards and so does giving yourself a hard time. It really is wasted emotion and wasted energy.

In the modern world, where communication is instant and harsh, there are more than enough opportunities in this world for other people to have a pop at us, so how about being a member of your own fan club instead of fight club. You really are a lot nicer than you might think you are.

21. WHERE DO YOU NEED TO SPEND MORE TIME IN REFLECTION?

When you ask people in the workplace how they are or how their work is going, you just never hear anyone say 'really easy going at the moment thanks' do you? We are all increasingly busy busy busy, a mass of busy bodies going from one task to another without a chance to draw breath. The business world has been talking about 'busy fools' for a long time now, and it seems that right now they're busier talking about them than ever. Where's Alanis Morissette when you need her?

I was speaking at a conference last year and I had the good fortune to listen to the presenter who was on stage before me and he was talking to the audience about, amongst other things, reflection time. I feel bad that I can't remember what some of those 'other things' were but the reflection component stuck with me for one simple reason: I needed to hear what he had to say and consider how to apply it to my world. The main idea that he was advocating to this business was to build in more reflection time in their working lives by creating gaps between one meeting and the next.

He proposed two changes to how they schedule their meetings: start every meeting on the hour and finish every meeting at a quarter to the hour. In his view, people rush from one meeting to the next without having had the chance to reflect on what took place during the earlier meeting, and as a result in many cases, taking some of the baggage from it into the following meeting.

What advantages can you think of by adopting this concept? You might be thinking, well what a waste of a quarter of your day, but have you ever had seven or eight hours choc-a-bloc full of meetings? By the end of the day your brain is mushed, struggling to remember who said what and to whom in which meeting, never mind trying to recall exactly what actions you committed to and by when.

I liked his idea and have really tried to apply it into my world but it's not easy for me. Reflection is something that I tend to do in tandem with another task, rather than give it my full attention. It's the brussels sprout of my working day – fine if you're eating it alongside something a bit more yummy, but a different proposition altogether if it's the only thing on your fork! How palatable would you find it? Where do you currently pause, reflect and digest before moving on to the next topic on your agenda? Where might you benefit from more reflection time, and what difference would it make to your contribution, your interactions and your productivity?

I'm not suggesting we all take on board the concept that I heard at the conference with immediate effect, but if it's not that, then when do we create time to look back before moving forward unabated? If you were to create 60 minutes every day to do just that, where would you find it? Stop sniggering at the back! OK, so how about 30 minutes? Fifteen? Ten minutes is my final offer before I snatch this book off you. On reflection, I've decided to let you continue but only because I know that if you stop and reflect for a moment then you'll be able to identify where you can factor time into your schedule to do just that for 10, 20 or 30 minutes every day. If the company I was delivering to can go way beyond that amount, then I don't think it's too much to ask, do you?

Supposing then that you decide to spend more time reflecting – what would you be reflecting on? To be clear, and without wishing to state the obvious, this is different from meditating, or just going quiet. When my wife goes quiet for a period of time I often ask her what she is thinking about. Invariably her short, sweet and swift response is 'nothing'. She's not reflecting, she's just gone silent for a while. It confuses the life out of me it has to be said, with our wildly opposing behavioural styles, but it suits her down to the ground.

Reflecting is when you take time to look back on what has gone, what has been said and done. It's when you consider the action or inaction that has taken place, identifying the successes that should be captured, bottled and repeated, and the 'failures' that should be analysed before identifying what changes could and should be made in the future. It's replaying the conversations that you engaged in, the role that you played and the difference that you made.

I bet there are not many days in the last few years where I've not visited Google Maps. Every new place that I plan to visit, personal and professional, gets typed in so that I can see exactly where it is located. On the first click it takes me straight to the exact location but it's the next few clicks when I start to get really excited (don't judge me – we all have our foibles!). The clicks where I start to zoom out and observe what is in the immediate vicinity and how far it is to walk to the other places that are close by. A few clicks down the line and I can see where that town is compared to the airport, or major cities. Oh the fun I have!

I do the same when reflecting and I've already revealed that I don't do that nearly often enough. I like to see how that one event fits with those events surrounding it then zoom out to consider its impact on my wider world, recognising that all those moments that we experience are connected in some way, we just might not know how yet.

When I design my training programmes I would benefit from letting my ideas incubate before sending the proposal to the client. There are times when I say yes to a request when, if I'd pressed pause for a while, I may well have arrived at the right answer that was no. On the occasions when I go to bed, turn off the light and my mind is like a hamster wheel, I should have taken time to untangle and unravel the knot of wool that was my day just gone.

On reflection there are plenty of occasions where I need to reflect more, and that's three that immediately came to mind. Have you reflected on yours? Don't answer just yet…

22. WHAT HAVE YOU NEVER DONE THAT YOU WOULD REALLY LIKE TO DO?

I've just signed up to do something that I've always wanted to do but in my view have never had the time nor the capacity to do. I'm going to walk coast to coast across England from west to east in one go. When I say one go, fear not, I will be getting my head down in various guest houses and inns along the way, but for 13 days I'll be traversing three famous northern National Parks, over hills and dales, selecting a pebble from one sea and rehoming it in the other.

I'm excited and apprehensive in equal amounts. Excited because the thought of setting a challenging goal and subsequently achieving it appeals to me immensely. Excited because my travelling companion is a blast from the past, reunited by our mutual passion for fresh air and fresh challenges, and two weeks in his company will be time incredibly well spent. And apprehensive because I've never walked nearly 200 miles before and my knees are already groaning at me five months prior to departure.

Never had the time nor the capacity? I bought all the maps that accompany those keen and daft enough to complete this walk 16 years ago and it's been in my mind a good deal longer than that. I've chosen to spend my time in other ways, I've chosen to spend my money on other things, and I've chosen to use the fact that no one was willing to partner me on my route as an excuse not to go for it. My choices and my excuses. What excuses are you making for not doing what you've always wanted to do? What did you choose to do instead of the activity that's occupying your mind in these first few paragraphs?

My trip is booked and a few moments after I parted with the money that ensured that beds and bars will be waiting for me at the end of each day and 'sherpas' will be transferring my bag each morning, I was sent information that reminded me that this was no straightforward task. There was a training plan! 'I haven't got time for that', I thought. They've already got two of my best weeks in the middle of the year, I had better earn some money at some point. For a brief moment I began to have doubts as to whether I really was in a position to pull this summer stroll off, and wondered whether I should just cut my losses and the deposit.

Thankfully that was short lived as I reminded myself that if you want to do something that you've never done (even though you've really wanted to) it comes at some kind of a cost. The word cost is often intrinsically linked to the financial outlays that we make yet it can be measured in so many forms of currency.

The cost for me is spending time heading up a few stiff hills in the early months of the year so that when I have to do the same day in day out in June and July it's no surprise to me mentally or physically. It's getting fitter, so I don't feel the urge to pack it in the minute the going starts to get tough. It's spending two weeks away from loved ones when I already spend a good proportion of my time away from home with my work. What would your cost be and is it a cost that you are prepared to make?

Would you *really* like to do it? I mean *really* or is it just something that you would like to do but aren't really that bothered if it happens or not? I'd like to fly in a helicopter but I had the chance to do just that while travelling in Australia recently and ended up doing something else with my time and money. If I had *really* wanted to do it then whatever it was that I did instead (visit a koala bear sanctuary if you're interested) would have been put on the back burner.

So once you've spent some time daydreaming about all the things you would like to do that you haven't done yet, write that list down then set about prioritising it so your cream rises to the top.

Struggling to think of anything? Then here's five questions that might stimulate you into putting pen to paper. What would give you the ultimate thrill? What are you scared to do but if you did it you would get an incredible buzz for having conquered your fears? What are you in a position to do now that you might not be in 20 years' time? What do you see other people doing and think to yourself 'I'd love to do that'? What experience would you share with anyone who would listen if you were to experience it?

As I write those questions, a myriad of thoughts are rushing through my head. I really want to jump out of an aeroplane, and as I consider my responses to those five questions they all point in that one direction – questions that five minutes ago I didn't know that I was going to pose you. For the sake of clarity, it might be worth pointing out to you that I also want to be accompanied on my jump by a parachute.

What answers spring to mind for you – five different and diverse ones or one big fat juicy one with your name on it sometime in the not too distant future? One that you really have always wanted to do but for some reason it has never materialised. Yet. Never say never.

I've shared with you a couple of fairly sizeable activities on my list, one that is imminent and one that I have no current plans for, but they don't all have to involve going further or higher than you've gone before. Some require small steps on your part. Talking of which, I want to be able to dance like they do on *Strictly Come Dancing* so the idea of having lessons puts a real spring in my step. Not quite the same adrenalin rush as the parachute jump but I'd still relish the opportunity. We've spoken about it for years but I've procrastinated due to being unable to make myself available on the same night of the week for a sustained period of time. Whether that's a reason or an excuse is up for debate. My dance partner is prepared to make the commitment so why can't I? It takes two to tango.

So what's stopping you doing what you would really like to do, assuming it's on the right side of the law, and what small steps could you take to edge you closer to ticking it off your list? Good luck, and maybe I'll see you on the dancefloor, up in the air, or somewhere in-between.

23. WHERE DO YOU NEED TO BE MORE ASSERTIVE?

Do you consider yourself to be an assertive person? I did. Then I met Barbara.

The first ever management training course that I attended was in the mid-90s. On the last day of the four-day workshop, the facilitator asked the group of 18 participants to rearrange themselves in the horseshoe of seats so that the most assertive person sat on the left of him and the least assertive sat on the right. I was fully aware of my positive contribution to the course by this stage, and having considered my peers and on watching them hesitate to find their chosen seat, I made my way to the seat furthest left. I was ready to claim my crown of Mr Assertive of Assertiveshire.

After what seemed an eternity the group were finally all sitting down and the facilitator asked a question that is as fresh today 25 years on as it was then. He simply enquired, "Does anyone think that someone is sitting in the wrong seat?" It was quiet for about 30 seconds when the lady sitting opposite me opened up. If you're wondering why I recall her name, she worked at Barclays and she was from the Blackpool branch so the alliteration stuck with me! Barbara gently said, "Yes, I think Mike is in the wrong seat." Immediately taken aback by her temerity, I was about to retort before she added, "I think that he is more aggressive than assertive."

I'm sure that my early foray into leadership development training was rich in material and learnings, but a quarter of a century on and it is this three-minute interlude that I still remember vividly as my take away from the week, and a lesson for life. The 'a-ha' for me was that my larger than life, ebullient nature can appear a tad overpowering to some, leaving them feeling undervalued or intimidated.

The reason that I decided to sit where I did was that I didn't see myself as submissive and my perception was that the people who were on the other side of the room from me were just that. Yet there are three components to my question: are you assertive, are you aggressive or are you submissive? If the answer to all three is sometimes, it depends or maybe, then stop sitting on the fence and for goodness sake give me an answer now! OK, maybe Barbara had a point, I'll stop that right there.

Which seat would you take up? Who would ask you to move down the assertiveness line and would it be because they saw you as more aggressive or submissive? As you consider my questions you might be asking yourself what definition we're using to help you make your decision. A quick search online would show you that there are a fair few out there but the simple premise is that assertive behaviour is standing up for yourself and your rights without denying the rights of others. Where might you benefit from doing just that, or if you focus on the second half of the statement, who else would benefit if this was the approach that you took?

When was the last time that you walked away from an interaction and thought to yourself 'that didn't go quite how I had planned'? The chances are that as you reflect on that encounter you may well have wished you'd have been more assertive.

There's no rocket science behind being assertive, and if you compare it to the other choices available, memories of reading

Goldilocks from your childhood may well come flooding back as you recall how the middle option is invariably the more appealing whether you're talking about porridge, beds or assertion.

Let's consider a few multiple choice situations to get a sense of where you're at. Are you afraid of speaking up, do you speak up too much and interrupt or do you speak openly about your thoughts and feelings? Is your voice too soft, too loud or just right, deploying a conversational tone? Do you avoid eye contact, stare too much or would you opt for somewhere in the middle of the two?

As you reflected on those three scenarios above, you probably knew which response fell under each of the three categories, so I sense you already know *how* to be assertive; the key is when and where you need to be. Who brings out the submissive part of you? Who do you struggle to articulate your point of view to, allowing them to feel like they've won while you walk away feeling like you've lost? How could you prepare for those interactions better?

No one can argue with how you feel, not even the person who you are thinking of right now. As you prepare yourself to express how you feel, consider the response that you might get. The reality is that response very rarely happens, and as with all walks of life, so much of what we worry about doesn't materialise. Where would you benefit from getting your voice heard more rather than suffering in silence, then walking away with festering resentment and potentially a victim mindset?

What about the other side of the border – the more aggressive side of assertive behaviour? Where might you benefit from allowing the other person or people to share the airspace? Where might you allow them to express how they feel? Where might you be a little more valuing and tolerant of their words, actions and concerns? Where might you seek to create win-win outcomes rather than having one member of the party walking away feeling hard done by? Who is your Barbara?

The thing is, Barbara was no lone voice. After she had been brave enough and bold enough, and how about assertive enough in speaking up as per the facilitator's request, he added, "Does anyone agree?" Nods, grunts and general signs of agreement resulted in me swapping seats with two thirds of the group as it transpired that my behaviour was viewed as largely aggressive by the majority of my fellow course participants.

Looking back, I can see why that was the perception. What could you do or should you do to change the perceptions that might exist about your assertive behaviour or the lack of it? You see how nicely I asked you – I'm getting there, slowly!

24. WHEN MIGHT LESS TALK AND MORE ACTION HOLD YOU IN GOOD STEAD?

Our garden is having a make-over. The tired-looking back of our house will soon be replaced with new this, that and the other as the decking gets replaced with a patio, a summer house replaces the boggy area in the bottom corner and mood lighting highlights the cleverly designed nooks and crannies. All resulting in a delightful setting to enjoy both day and night. I know this because we made this decision six years ago. Do me a favour though and don't come and pay me a visit any time soon to admire my herbaceous borders because we've not started. It's been discussed more times than I've mowed the lawn in those six years and yet I still look out of the back window and see a garden that provides no pleasure and continues to look at its best under six inches of snow, that great leveller in gardening circles.

On a recent visit my mother enquired, "I thought you said that you were going to make your garden look nice – have you changed your mind?" Bless her, there's been no change of plan, we've just never pulled our finger out, or spade for that matter. We did get as far as having a gardener come round and take a look, not that he'll remember. He's probably been too busy dealing with those customers who put their money where their mouth was. I use the word we but that's being unfair on Mrs Jones as the garden is and always has been my domain. She sits out in it in the summer, but in the allocated responsibilities of our domesticity, anything green has my name on it (unless it's in the fridge).

'You're all talk and no action!' Has that one ever been levelled at you? As put downs go it's always been a tough one to be on the receiving end of. Yet in the case of my lawn and its surrounds it's a criticism that I need to take fairly and squarely on the chin. Where might it be relevant in your world? Where have you flattered to deceive with your over promising and under delivering? What have you been talking about doing for what seems like an eternity but the words have never quite translated into anything tangible or resembled anything like progress? There are two ways in which you can address this words versus action imbalance: you could back up the verbals with activity or you could simply reduce them – which is it to be?

For many years I've talked about writing a book, mentioning it to anyone either prepared to listen or happening to be in earshot. I discussed it with so many people that I actually forgot who knew of my plans and who didn't. "How's that book coming along?" they would ask, knowing full well that it hadn't left the starting block. Then five months ago I made the decision to only talk about what was still to come on this project if it could be prefixed with what had actually been achieved to date. The action increased and the words decreased and as the balance tipped so the task progressed.

You might not be writing a book but what have you spoken about doing but, alas, have no activity to update anyone on? If you were to bump into someone in a month's time, and they enquired about that something that you had previously brought up in a conversation with them, what would you be telling them that they didn't already know? The progress report is that there has been no progress. Not so impressive, hey?

If you stop and think for a minute about the conversations that you've had over the last week, how many times can you recall that you've either intimated, stated or even promised that you would take action? If you've got a 50% success rate of following through on your actions then you're probably doing better than most, but what is stopping us from actually doing what we say we are going to do? At best it's forgetful and at worst it's unreliable or untrustworthy. Not the most pleasant of traits for people to remember you for.

Let's think about some of those areas where you might have done just that. The phone call that you said you would make, the email that you said you would send, the errand that you said you would run, meeting up with a friend for a gym trip or to see the latest film. If you know that the chances of carrying out your commitment are slim, then why say it or write it in the first place? Who might you have left hanging, wondering what better offer you had received?

Now don't get me wrong here, I'm firmly a member of the 'it's good to talk' fan club, fully paid up since the day that my mouth was able to make coherent noises. So please don't read this and think that the insertion of a sock to plug the erroneous hole is the answer. Keep on making conversation, giving your opinion, showing interest and passing the time of day. Just challenge yourself to ensure that your words are backed up with actions when the words chosen suggest that an action is imminent. What a great reputation to have – someone who does what they say they are going to do. Someone who is true to their word.

I reckon that we all say we'll do something far more than we would like to think. Set yourself a task for the next week. Write down everything that you say you're going to do. Discipline yourself to get your notebook out at the end of every conversation or meeting. Then tick off the ones that you have taken action on. My bet is that the very fact you do this means that you will act on more of your commitments.

True to your word – wow, that's a powerful statement isn't it? I think we'd all like a slice of that. Get it right and everything in your garden will be rosy. Mine, however, might just take a little bit longer!

25. WHO ENABLES YOU TO SEE THE WORLD DIFFERENTLY?

Wouldn't life be just a little bit boring if we were all the same? I love the phrase 'my other half' – three little words that mean so much, suggesting that we are only a half of a whole and need someone else to complete our circle. This is a wonderfully Jungian phrase and it goes way beyond the person who you may have chosen to spend your life with. My interpretation is that your other half is that person who possesses all those ingredients and gifts that you don't happen to have in your own kitbag and so what a relief it is when someone comes along with them in abundance, saving you the trouble of having to acquire them yourself!

What are those attributes that you might be missing yet you value so highly in others? I really appreciate people who are wonderfully relaxed. I look on admiringly at the strong, silent type, having known for years that I'm not that strong and I'm not that silent. I am in awe of those who can evaluate a problem logically before arriving at a considered solution that actually solves the problem in question. As I type those words people in my network come into my head from past and present, and as they do I recognise that these are just some of the many people that I come into contact with who enable me to see the world differently.

When I turn to them to pour my heart out, vent my spleen or offer my emotive opinion they say things that I wouldn't say, do things I wouldn't do and generally look at the issue from a different angle.

Not the right angle, not the wrong angle, a different angle. They enable me to see the world differently.

As I write these words I'm on a flight heading back from Istanbul where I have been working with a marketing department, and what a mighty fine bunch they were. There were 38 participants and as diverse a group as you could wish to meet – by age, gender, experience, colour, ethnicity and behaviour. What a joy to have 18 different nationalities represented, and what a relief I might add that English was the common language otherwise I would have been in a bit of a muddle! They saw the world differently, and even more importantly, they were willing to listen and learn from the differences that existed within their peers. There are three stages to this: firstly you need to recognise that the differences exist, then you need to value those differences and only then can you use the differences to your advantage.

This particular marketing team were seeking to use their differences to be more innovative and more competitive. In your relationships what would the benefit be to you? How about being more informed, more educated, more tolerant or more aware? Add to that list if you can and you'll see that the benefits of spending time in the presence of those who enable you to see the world differently far outweigh the drawbacks. Hang on, what are the drawbacks? Nope, I can't think of any either.

I reckon that these people are wide and varied in your world. Consider your friends, your colleagues, your customers and your family. My eldest daughter, long referred to by her younger siblings as my favourite, is a complex and beautiful individual who never ceases to intrigue me, push my boundaries and warm my heart with her quirky approach to life. She enables me to see the world differently. So does my best friend. Reserved, risk-averse and consistent – if I'm his chalk then he is most definitely my cheese. And if you think they're similar try writing on a board with a wedge of brie.

An ex-colleague who is now one of my favourite people in the world is everything that I am not. She challenges me, stretches me and has a totally different approach to decision making, relationships and living her life from mine. Different? You could say that. All three are different and all three are special to me, and I'm grateful and comforted by the fact that they provide me with a different lens to go world gazing with.

Let's take the four benefits I mentioned a moment ago and see who enables you to be more of each. Who makes you more informed? Who is that person who has a different view from you, a view based on insight and experience, and as a result of them sharing it with you it provides you with additional information on which to view the world?

Who enables you to be more educated? We all have those brainy friends who just seem to have a greater ability to store knowledge, but the reality is it is merely different, additional knowledge from what you have gained on your travels. This knowledge stuff has the habit of growing if you allow yourself to spend time with those that enable you to see the world differently.

What about tolerant? I say tolerant as there may have been a time when their differences would have irritated you and you might have rejected their point of view without thought. Yet now it has made you more accepting of people who hold similar thoughts or who demonstrate similar behaviours to them. You've become more tolerant of those who are not like you as a result. And finally, who enables you to be more self-aware – that person who challenges your thoughts, actions and emotions and holds a mirror up to you so you can see what others can see?

Hopefully you've got at least four names, one for each of those categories. Now why don't you go and thank them for helping to make you an even better person? Tell them why that's the case and provide examples. The reassuring thing is, if they're reading this book then they are probably thinking about you as they reflect on the questions posed in this chapter – it's a two-way street. And if they're not reading this book then the least you can do is recommend it to them. After all, I'm trying my hardest here to enable you to see the world differently!

26. WHEN DO YOU FEEL TEN FEET TALL?

How tall are you? Without your shoes and resisting the urge to stand on your tip-toes how tall actually are you? I'm just short of five foot nine inches so by my reckoning that leaves me 51 inches short of the ten-foot mark, and I reckon that you are probably between 40 and 60 inches short of that margin too. In fact, a quick look at *Guinness World Records* reveals that no one has ever reached such lofty heights given the same constraints that I gave you.

But how tall you are and how tall you feel are two quite different measurements. So when do you feel ten feet tall regardless of how short of the mark you might be in reality? When is it that you feel like a giant, feeling mighty fine about who you are and what you've achieved? That's a good feeling isn't it? That sense of invincibility, that feeling that you are on top of the world, or a good few inches closer to it than normal. Whether it be your accomplishments, your environment or the company that you're keeping, it's vital that we can all capture and bottle those feelings as you never know when you might need to remind yourself of the experience, drawing on your reserves to either snap yourself out of a lull or to repeat more of the same.

I feel ten feet tall when a big audience responds to one of my presentations with a rousing round of applause as it reaches its conclusion. It doesn't happen every time I can tell you, so when I am faced with one of the more challenging groups it's these memories that give me the strength to believe in my own abilities. I feel ten feet tall when I venture into the country and climb somewhat higher than that. As I stand on top of a mountain or way up above civilisation, I take in my surroundings using all of my senses and feel inspired by the world and how lucky I am to be a part of it. I felt ten feet tall as I watched my three daughters all graduate, physically growing in stature (albeit with a tissue in hand) as they strode up to be acknowledged for their endeavours.

What accomplishments of yours have given you a similar feeling? Where do you go to grow in size? How do the loved ones that you surround yourself with have the same impact on you? All three have the same impact, the one where you can literally feel yourself standing taller, prouder and just that bit more invincible.

It's a wonderful feeling isn't it? Far better don't you think than the other end of the spectrum where you feel two-foot tall? The feeling of worthlessness, that imposter syndrome that we all get from time to time. That feeling of stupidity. One way that we can spend more time feeling ten feet tall is to remove the two-foot shackles. Spend less time feeling small and you increase your chances of feeling big. Who are those people that make you feel better about who you are and the contribution that you make? My advice is simple: surround yourself with people who make you feel good about yourself.

I used to use the same taxi driver for my airport drop-offs and pick-ups. Given that I'm there with great regularity we got to know each other fairly well and shared mutual hobbies so we were never short of something to discuss en route. We became Facebook Friends which meant that he would get to see more of my life than the 25-minute chatter that accompanied every trip to and from home. For whatever reason he appeared quite interested in my posts and was never short of an opinion on what I was up to and where I was going.

Humorous at first, his words gradually became more cutting until it became a frequent occurrence that he would criticise my comments, photos and whatever I chose to add.

"I've never met anyone who posts as many pictures of themselves – look at me aren't I great, look where I am in the world now," he scathingly commented during one unpleasant journey. It wasn't particularly uplifting to be on the receiving end of when all I was doing was paying for a lift. When I arrived home I was beginning to question my approach to social media, having always been really mindful not to look boastful about all those aspects of my life that give me such pleasure. I shared the story with other friends and family and they all concurred that this was a combination of jealousy and bitterness at play on his part.

I didn't need it and having reflected on the relationship decided that this was not someone that I needed to spend time with, striving to bring me closer to two-foot than ten-foot. I deleted him as a 'friend' and used another taxi company from that point on. Choose your taxi driver carefully, and your friends, and your colleagues, and how you spend your time for that matter.

So who are those people that are quick to spot your qualities, willing to accept your shortcomings, and willing to give you nudges in the right direction with nothing other than positive intentions? Get them in the diary more than they currently are as these people create a feel-good factor in you long after they've left the room. They give you a lift and I don't mean to the airport. You might not like to stride uphill in the way that I do, but if it's not doing that then what are you doing when you feel ten-foot tall? Whether it's playing or praying, cooking or coaching, remind yourself why you feel so good about yourself when you are participating in your chosen act.

I reckon we're all ten-foot tall – we just spend too much time trying to put ourselves down or allowing others to do the same. Stick your chest out, push those shoulders back, grab yourself some stepladders if you must – however you do it, reach that rounded number that often gets referred to yet we spend little time touching.

But don't stand on your tip-toes remember, that would be cheating.

27. WHAT DO YOU NEED TO SIMPLIFY?

Simple – has there ever been a more subjective word in the dictionary? When I open the bonnet of my car and see an intricate web of machinery parts laughing back at me I don't know where to start. All I wanted to do was top up the washer bottle so I could see through my windscreen. Yet when the car visited the garage recently for its annual service the guy in the overalls salivated as he peered into the same area. He knows his way around an engine and to him it's 'simple' to be able to deduce exactly what is wrong and what to do about it. What's that phrase – one man's meat is another man's poison? So in this context we could say one person's simple is another person's mind-numbingly difficult.

For this question however, when looking for the polar opposite of simple let's go with the word complex rather than difficult, although a thesaurus would probably throw up a few more than that (it's not that simple really).

What do you find really simple about your life? What are those aspects of your routine that you could do with your eyes closed (sleep not included)? I'm a contact lens wearer and when I was sharing a room on a recent boys' trip my mate said, "How do you manage to do that twice a day – it looks really fiddly?" It's been said before by those who have never had to mess around with their eyes in what looks like a mini laboratory, yet to me, 35 years a contact lens wearer, I could do it with my eyes closed. Hang on, I need to simplify that statement – it's second nature. What do you find simple that others might not?

Now consider what seems all a bit too confusing, too time consuming, or that word complex. To be clear, I have no real desire to attend a crash course on car maintenance (come to think of it, a 'crash course' might not be their best seller). I'm content knowing that there is somewhere that I can go that is populated with experts in that area. So let's focus on those areas that are down to you and you alone – you can't just farm them off on someone else. Which areas could you benefit from making just that little bit more simple?

How does that period look between rising from your slumber and settling into your work on an average weekday morning? Plenty of time to wake slowly, leisurely breakfast with loved ones discussing plans for the day and beyond? Is it a serene dream or a cacophony of chaos? What tweaks could you make so that you're not left shattered before your day has left the starting block?

Every time I deliver a workshop there are a number of distinct stages and the two main components I like to think that I am pretty competent at. When it comes to both the design and delivery of the solution my approach works, both for me and for the client. Another stage however isn't quite so smooth – preparing to depart the home as I head off on my travels. My job has required me to travel near and far for the last 28 years yet still the packing of my bag is a process that, on every occasion, appears like it is my maiden voyage and my first encounter with that oblong thing known as a suitcase. I frantically try to remember all my lotions and potions while causing a commotion. My mind runs through the itinerary for the trip as I consider what clothes need to be packed: is it business, business casual, casual, ridiculously casual? For goodness sake man, make a decision!

The various materials that are required for my session are randomly gathered from behind more doors, drawers, cupboards and shelves than I can cope with, and nothing ever, and I mean ever, seems to go back from wherever it came. I really need to simplify my approach to leaving home for a few days, for my benefit and anyone else's benefit who happens to come into contact with the temporary whirling dervish.

How does your lack of 'simple' impact those around you and what might you do to reduce that impact? Where might the odd process contribute to you maintaining your composure and being able to put your finger on anything and everything that you would much prefer not to lose? We all have a useful drawer in the home – that place where really important 'bits and bobs' are placed to ensure that we never lose them. What was the last thing that you thought was in that drawer but it wasn't? Ours was the glue that we use to fix things. We lost that last week. I could have sworn it was in the useful drawer. What have you recently lost and what would have helped you to have been able to put your finger on it at any point (ah yes, isn't hindsight a wonderfully irritating thing?).

I need to find a place for everything so everything has its place. Currently there is a place for everything and everything is all over the place. Can you relate to that or are you actually a very tidy person so this chapter doesn't apply to you? Well simple doesn't just mean tidy, so what are those aspects of your day or your life that would benefit from greater simplicity? Is it your work, your relationships or your finances? If that was met with a 'no, no, no' then what option would be met with a 'yes'?

So often in the workplace there are processes that have been in place for years – processes that add no value but help to create a consistency of approach. It reminds me of a story that I used to share with great regularity when my focus in the workplace was to help teams balance effectiveness with efficiency. Let me share that story with you, and I'll try to keep it short and sweet... and simple.

A woman was cooking Sunday roast for her family when her child noticed her cutting both ends of the roast off and tossing them into the bin before she put the meat in the oven. The child questioned why this was being done and her mother merely said, "That's a secret family recipe – cut both ends off and smother the new ends in special herbs and seasoning."

The child thought nothing of it until she went for Sunday dinner at her grandmother's house. The same secret recipe was carried out much to the child's amusement and pleasure. Then on a subsequent visit to her great grandmother she asked her elderly family member if she would cook her the traditional family roast. She obliged and was just about to put the meat in the oven when the child said, "Great Grandma, you've forgotten to cut both ends off – the secret family recipe, remember?" The great grandmother laughed as she replied, "They're not still doing that are they? I used to do that, but then I bought a bigger tin."

What do you do because you've always done it, and how could you simplify your processes?

By the way, I can now easily locate the washer bottle under my bonnet. I hadn't realised but there is a picture of a windscreen on the cap. Simple really.

28. HOW GOOD A FRIEND ARE YOU AND HOW COULD YOU BECOME AN EVEN BETTER ONE?

The word friend has changed shape over the last ten years or so to include those people who you might never have met but have invited you to be their 'friend' on social media. On Instagram you are often given offers enticing you to buy followers so why not buy friends? Life would be so much easier if you didn't have to bother finding people whose company you enjoy, people that you can be your authentic self with, and people that you share mutual hobbies and interests with. Easier maybe but a whole lot less meaningful.

Who are your friends? If you had to count how many you have, what number would it equate to? When I work with groups looking at their behavioural similarities or differences I ask them to respond to a series of statements, one of which is 'do you perceive that you have a wide circle of friends and acquaintances?' As a rule of thumb the more extroverted amongst them tend to respond positively whereas the more introverted shake their heads. Their focus tends to be on depth rather than breadth.

Whether you're a wider or deeper kind of person, consider who would class you as their friend, and is it the same people that you came up with when answering the same question? It really all boils down to what defines a friend and we all have our own definition. What's yours? Here are five to get you started. Someone who listens to you and your issues, free from judgment. Someone who revels in your successes and is there for you in your failures. Someone who, despite the fact that it has seemed an eternity since you last saw or heard from them, you can carry on with from where you left off with no guilt on the table. Someone that you can trust with your secrets, whatever they are. Someone that is comfortable sharing silences with you. When thinking of those people you consider to be your friends, what are the other additions to that quintet?

How do you show up against that friendship five? How effective are you at listening to your friends? Do they come to you with their issues or are they more likely to confide in others for one reason or another – the counsel they would give, the fact that it wouldn't go any further or that they would be sure of an empathic response? Judgment has received a bad press over the years but we all need to convey judgment; however, it crosses the line when it becomes judgmental. To help you with your self-assessment here, judgment is passing a view based on the evidence available, being judgmental is having a view on an individual because of the evidence. Where are you on that sliding scale?

Who are your cheerleaders and whose cheerleader are you? If someone in your circle wanted to be reminded of how wonderful they are, would they come to you? Who comes to you to share their successes? When they do are you thrilled for them or is there a part of you that has a pang of jealousy or resentment? I bet your first reaction to that challenge is an unequivocal no. Of course it is, isn't it? What about the harder times – are you there then as a shoulder to cry on, comfortable in those times to hear more about their woes rather than sharing your own news items, and in doing so giving them the air time that they temporarily crave?

People often cite that the sign of a good friendship is one where you can just carry on where you left off. I fully subscribe to that view, but on recent occasions I have been left wondering why it was ever left so long in the first place. If you are under the age of 30 it might sound strange but I first wrote the letters 'www' at the age of 31 and owned my first mobile phone two years later. Having grown up in an age where communication was never quite so instantaneous, one of the great joys that the much maligned social media can bring is that it can reconnect you with people who you have lost touch with. Thirty years on from being thick as thieves, a group of likely lads did just that as we reunited and carried on as if we'd never been apart. Five minutes in and 'you've not changed' was given its first airing as we laughed, joked, shared stories and updated each other on the last 1,500 weeks of our lives.

Think of those folk who you still class as a friend but in reality they've barely been seen or heard of in recent memory. Why is that? Oh I know – you're both busy. Well maybe they might just need you in their world right now but don't want to just make contact out of the blue because they are a friend in need. So why don't you be a friend indeed and reach out to some of those stragglers? Check in with them, see how they are.

I've said it in previous chapters and I'll no doubt be saying it again but we all have the same amount of time in our week and we all have a choice of how we spend it. What are you doing that's potentially getting in the way of being the type of friend to others that you would like to be on the receiving end of?

At the turn of the millennium, as I entered the period that I now refer to as my in-between wives phase, I was desperate for friendship – people who would understand my pain and cajole me into facing the world with renewed vim and vigour. I had some great nights out in that time, but what I really wanted and needed was a break. The sad thing was that I couldn't find a single friend to go away with – not for a weekend and not for a week. I was on my own. I wouldn't want one of my friends to feel like that. Would you?

Someone needs your support, love, camaraderie and friendship right now, so in 30 seconds you can stop reading this chapter and remind them why they thought so much of you in the first place to bestow that most precious title on you. A title that is open to interpretation but only ever has a positive intention – their friend. Do you know who it is?

29. WHAT DO YOU NEED TO START SAYING NO TO A BIT MORE OFTEN?

There's an exercise that I use when delivering workshops on the subject of change where I get people to partner up and take it in turns to ask each other a series of closed questions. If they answer 'yes' then they need to shake their head when they provide their response, and likewise when they answer with a 'no' they have to nod their head. This is done to raise the issue that one definition of change is breaking old comfortable habits and developing new, initially uncomfortable ones. Give it a try and you'll see what I mean.

Yes and no – two little words that tend to get uttered rather a lot by all of us. Two words in some ways connected but totally opposite. Reflect for a moment if you will on the last few hours and recall what you have said yes to. Was that your answer to any of these? 'Have you finished with this?' 'Is this seat available?' 'Does this look OK?' or 'Fancy going for a drink later?' We forget how often we say it but it's probably up there with the 'ands' and 'the's' of the world as one of our most spoken words.

More I would suggest than its much maligned opposite. 'No? What do you mean no?' We live in a world where we are coerced into having a can-do mentality where the answer is 'yes, now what's the question?' Don't get me wrong, I'm all for a bit of 'can-do' but what I'd like you to consider over these next few pages is what should you be saying no to a bit more often instead of saying yes reluctantly for a range of reasons. Reasons such as not wanting to let someone down perhaps, or because of what people might think of you, or because everyone else has said yes.

When did you say yes, when on reflection you should have said no? When, having agreed to something, were you left shortly afterwards pondering 'why did I just say that?' That extra work you agreed to, that you knew would make you late home or put you under unnecessary pressure when your to-do list was already overflowing? Spending money on that purchase that you might have wanted but didn't really need, when the outlay would have been put to better use elsewhere? Or perhaps agreeing to a night on the tiles when what was really wanted or needed was a quiet night in? Just think of what some of the benefits could have been for actually providing the answer that you really wanted to give but didn't for concern as to how it would be received.

I love a good night out, and I'm partial to an impromptu spending spree, oh and my to-do list only ever seems to grow so we need to keep this real. I'm not saying replace all your nods with shakes but where do you need to start saying it a bit more often? I'm trying to lose weight so I need (and choose) to say it when people ask me if I want another slice or another round. The work/life balance that we all seek is currently making me question the feasibility of taking on every project that has revenue-generating possibilities. There's a clothing brand that I've recently started wearing, so much so that I've purchased six different T-shirts in a short space of time. I need to start saying no a bit more otherwise my wardrobe is going to look like a factory outlet for said brand. That's three of mine – one each for health, work and finances. What's on your list and which aspects of your world would benefit from the additions of a few more no's?

A yes/no answer is a response to different types of questions. In its simplest form the other person is seeking information, and in this instance saying no when the answer is yes isn't really going to help. At best it would be confusing and at worst you would quickly get a reputation for telling porkies!

Then it can also be used to solicit your opinion – do you like this television programme, is that tasty, do you think the government is doing a good job, and should the police be armed? As you can see some might require a bit more thought than others, but they're opinion-providing responses all the same.

The third area is the one where you are probably looking to increase the no count – the decision-making section. How many decisions have you taken today where you absolutely had a choice? It will run into three figures every day I guarantee you, as we spend a good proportion of our time making decisions: where to go, when to go, who to go with, what to spend our time doing, how much to spend, how long to spend etc.

Many of these, however, are just decisions that we make without input from others. When I work from home I decide that I am going to make myself a cup of tea so I venture into the kitchen and put the kettle on. I open the fridge to retrieve the milk that I've decided to add to the tea and decide to eat a couple of mouthfuls of last night's left-overs. I decide to put the television on and choose to remain there flicking through channels for ten minutes. There's a handful of decisions being made in that one paragraph and no one is any the wiser.

But what about the ones where others are involved? 'Please could you give me a lift to the station later?' You've got a whole range of choices there haven't you? Do it gladly, do it reluctantly, don't do it, decline and offer an alternative solution. Feeling that you have a choice is a wonderfully liberating mindset to have. But do you?

Why do you feel manipulated into saying yes when you really want to say no? This isn't meant to be a lesson in how to say no, rather encouraging you to consider where you need to start doing it, but if you're looking for a few quick pointers here are three strategies that will set you on your way.

Firstly, the good old broken record technique has been lauded in assertion circles for many a year and it works. Repeat the same response on several occasions without necessarily using exactly the same words. Be clear with your message that no is a no on this occasion.

Secondly, look the other party in the eye when saying no. Smile if you need to while you're at it (without gloating!) conveying the sense that you've arrived at your decision and you're confident and content with it – it's nothing personal but that's the answer.

Thirdly, be clear on your rationale for your 'no' response. You don't have to share it with those who might have been looking for the alternative answer, but having clarity in your own mind and a reason that can be delivered if called on will hold you in good stead.

Time to put some of this chapter into practice I reckon – ready to start straight away? What do you mean no? Wow – you're a quick learner!

30. WHAT IS YOUR GREATEST STRENGTH THAT YOU'RE NOT CURRENTLY MAKING USE OF?

I used to love playing team sports. I was never the best nor the strongest, the fastest nor the most skilful, but there was a reason why I was captain of the three football teams that I played with for over a period of 15 consecutive years. I was good at the captaincy bit. In fact, I once got voted man of the match in a game where I barely touched the ball. My contribution was to get the best out of the others, motivate them to give their all for the cause, shout praise from the rooftops and distribute rollickings at close quarters in order to ensure that, individually and collectively, we played to the best of our ability.

Nostalgia, hey? It's not what it used to be. I've just read that first paragraph back and the memories of my 90s sporting prowess come flooding back. Good grief, we were hopeless but we didn't half enjoy ourselves! The last time I played a competitive game of football or cricket, the two team sports that filled both my diary and washing machine, was in 2000. As my first marriage came to an end so did the way that I spent my weekends. It's been 19 years since I've shared the camaraderie of the dressing room and I do miss it. I miss it a lot.

That's not surprising really because if you're good at something and you stop doing it, it's highly likely that you'll miss it. Nothing has ever replaced the pleasure that I got from captaining the team and I reckon that some teams could have benefited over the years from my mixture of passion and determination, with a good dose of the gift of the gab thrown in for good measure. It was a strength of mine, and although in my work I spend time helping teams become more effective in a whole manner of ways, I'm not a part of any of those teams. It's a strength of mine that is not currently being utilised. Not currently and not for a long time.

What strength of yours are you not making use of? Whether at work or in your personal life as you consider your passions and pastimes, experiences and expertise, what are you pretty good at but the world isn't currently gaining either exposure to or benefit from? Is that a waste? Is that a shame? Is that something that you would like to address?

I had to make choices back then. I could have continued playing if I had stopped watching Manchester United, my number one passion. That was never really going to be an option though, some switches you just can't flick on and off, so the extra Daddy time was created by releasing my captaincy duties. It may well be that you're not making use of your strength because your time was required elsewhere and that's understandable and commendable. My story, however, takes me back two fifths of my life – how far are you going back and have times changed? On reflection, could you start making more use of that strength that was put on the back burner for whatever reason?

I was walking my dog down by the riverside recently one Saturday and, as is often the case at the weekend, it was populated with rowers (the boat kind not the argumentative kind). There is a rowing club based there and the usual combination of single rowers and teams of various sizes were all gliding through the water with effortless speed. Now far be it from me to stick my oar in but they really seemed to be enjoying themselves and it left me contemplating what came first. No, not the chicken or the egg but the capability or the enjoyment. Did they become good at something because they enjoyed doing it or did they enjoy doing it because they were good at it?

Consider some of your strengths for a moment and which of those two came first? What do you enjoy doing because you excel in that area? What did you used to really enjoy doing because you were skilled at it, and if you picked up where you left off would that skill still be there waiting and willing to be dusted down? On the flip side what did you enjoy doing and as a result became fairly accomplished in that area? I used to love telling jokes, always ready and willing to provide an impromptu quip. It was something that I revelled in and it wasn't until a good few years later that I got paid to make an audience laugh for the first time.

Don't get too excited – my career as a stand-up comedian was over before it began due to a harrowing experience at a rugby tournament where the audience much preferred to be the stars of their own show. This ability slotted fairly and squarely into the 'enjoyment first, competence second' category, and as I reflect on my past I question why I allowed one challenging experience to put me off something that provided me with such pleasure, and I had some modicum of talent at.

What stopped you and what is stopping you from rekindling that strength of yours? Professionally what did you get paid to do that you no longer do, and personally what used to fill both your diary and your heart because you wanted it to? What did you receive appreciation, acknowledgement and accolades for, and as you reflect on past times it puts a smile on your face and a spring in your step as much now as it did back then?

We don't have to dig deep into the annals of time though. Consider something that you have recently done that you don't ordinarily spend all your time doing where you were left thinking to yourself 'I should do more of that'. What was it that you enjoyed about it and got either a warm glow or an even warmer buzz from? Let's forget about you for a minute and how you might want to be spending your time and consider the rest of the world; which strength of yours would they benefit from you making greater use of, whether that strength is a blast from the past or a recent revelation?

I'm not a fan of the phrase 'use it or lose it' – those strengths of yours have not disappeared forever never to be seen again, but they sure aren't helping anyone, least of all yourself, stuck in the cupboard gathering dust. Ah the cupboard – I wonder if that's where I'll find my old captain's armband?

31. WHAT DO YOU NEED TO WORRY LESS ABOUT?

I'm worried about this chapter. I'm worried that I haven't got enough to say on this subject and worried that you won't get much benefit from it. I'm worried that I'm running out of ideas as I let my fingers just type whatever comes into my mind without planning or preparation. I'm worried that the words I choose to use aren't big enough or maybe they're too big. I don't want to come across as either too simplistic or pompous. In fact, I'm worried about how much I'm worried about, which in itself is worrying.

Am I alone here or is that a snapshot of where you sometimes find yourself – in a downward worry spiral? We all do it, at different times, for different reasons and with different levels of intensity but we all do it none the less. Stop and think for a moment about the thoughts that occupy your mind that would populate your 'worry zone'. What are you currently worrying about? I have some good news for you: 85% of those things are never going to happen. Not now and not ever.

If you don't believe me then cast your mind back to some of your more recent worries. Remember that night out that you worried about or that exam? How about coming face to face with that person or that meeting you were attending? You worried about your loved ones doing what they were doing, going where they were going and spending time with who they were spending time with and most of these worries were unfounded, weren't they? Those dark thoughts that were at the front and centre of your mind never actually took place – 85% of them at least.

In case you're wondering (or worrying), I haven't plucked that percentage figure from thin air; there's been a whole myriad of studies that have taken place over the years by people far more knowledgeable on the topic than me, and whilst that figure fluctuates slightly depending on which expert you listen to, the sentiment is the same. My focus is to ask you some questions that get you thinking and moving rather than doing my own in-depth analysis on the science of worry, so let me ask you, what are you worrying about that you shouldn't be? What takes up vital space in your head and your heart – space that would be put to more effective use on issues that are far more pleasant and productive to occupy your time?

As you reflect on what some of these space invaders might be, consider which of these three categories they fit into: those that you have total control over; those that you can influence; and those that you have no control over whatsoever.

Apparently, one of the biggest things that we worry about is that we will be late and the main element of that is that we will oversleep (oh how I wish!). If that's you then let's start with a simple question: is that something you can control? If your answer is no, then I'm alarmed and so should you be. I mean, you should purchase one of those clocks that makes such a noise (at the time of your choice) that your chances of remaining in the land of nod are reduced somewhat. You have control over how much you pay for this sleep-reducing device, and what shape, size and colour you want it to be. You also have a choice as to what time you would like it to spring into life.

So, given that you have complete control over this I put it to you that you have no need to worry about oversleeping. One down off your worry list and 226 to go? If that is the case, then go through this extensive list and identify how many fit into the same category as the sleep scenario. You really do have a lot more control than you might think you have.

I used to worry that I would miss flights so I started leaving for the airport earlier. I used to worry that I would run out of the tablets that I need to take on a daily basis so I started collecting them from the pharmacist earlier in the month. I used to worry that I'd pull a muscle on the treadmill so I started doing stretches before I began. In case you're thinking 'well bully for you, smarty pants', there's a whole load that I still need to work on, don't you worry! What could you do to help yourself worry less?

In his book *The Seven Habits of Highly Effective People* Dr Stephen Covey referred to two circles: the circle of concern and the circle of influence. As he did so he identified two types of people: those who are reactive and those who are proactive. Reactive people, he said, focus their efforts in the circle of concern and these tend to be things that, as mentioned earlier, they have no control over. The weather would be a good example of this. Form an orderly queue behind me on that one – I'm way out in front! Proactive people, however, focus their efforts in the circle of influence, working on things that they can do something about.

Let's take two of the biggest sources of worry here: health and money. If you are worried about your health, you can influence that. Your financial situation? Yep, you can influence that too. You may well be rejecting those pithy sentences at this point, but with the right help and advice, and a good dose of willpower, determination and focus you can. What are you currently worried about that would fit into the circle of influence? And if that is the circle that it's firmly nestled in, then what are you doing about it to reduce your concerns?

You really are more influential than you probably think you are and more pessimistic than you need to be. Michel De Montaigne, the writer and philosopher, put pen to paper nearly 500 years ago and one of his more well-documented musings was 'My life has been filled with terrible misfortune – most of which never happened.' You see they were doing it way back then and we still haven't learned our lesson! I reckon he mixed in some pretty impressive circles, maybe he needed to mix more in the circle of influence rather than the circle of concern.

Take charge of your own worries, your own life and your own destiny and I reckon you'll have a lot less to lie awake at night about, whether you set that alarm clock or not.

32. WHAT ADVICE WOULD THE TEENAGE VERSION OF YOU GIVE YOU?

There was an iconic programme on television in the UK a few years back which made people laugh and squirm in equal measure, such was its accurate and uncomfortable portrayal of those in-between years that we all pass through – the segue between childhood and adulthood. The years when you know the answer to everything and nothing simultaneously.

These years often get derided, particularly by those of us who have long since experienced them with varying degrees of success, but maybe we could learn a lot from their combination of cavalier, curious and innocent approach to taking on the world. Think back to your teenage years, those six years in your life that ended with the same four letters that helped put you on the map, gave you a voice, and allowed you to push the boundaries as you sought to identify your own version of what was right and wrong, good and bad, pleasant and unpleasant.

Undoubtedly some of your behaviour and perceptions of the world will be unrecognisable to you now. Your wardrobe and record collections might cause some nostalgic merriment, and the old photographs might have you breathing a sigh of relief that social media hasn't always been there to capture every minute of every day. Yet if you take time to reflect on the person that was you, just a younger version, they might just be worth listening to. Might they have some advice for you that could help you as you continue unabated on the rest of your journey? The same journey but a few miles down the road? I reckon they could you know!

When I was 13 I wasn't that concerned with what people thought I looked like. If I glanced in the mirror and thought 'you look great' that did it for me. The 15-year-old version of me had no fear – nothing was too hard, too high, too dangerous, too anything. As a 17-year-old, I had a swagger, a confidence that any room I walked into was lucky to have me. Fast forward two years and the 19-year-old was continuously searching for meaning, the next thing that would help climb the ladder, not of success necessarily but of life. Wow, that was a cathartic five minutes that I've just had! If you were to erase the words that were personal to me and replace them with your own, how would this paragraph read?

That was me in the odd years of my teenage life (see what I did there?). That is the person that I recollect, so the question is what advice would they provide me with? Right now, 13-year-old Mike would say why always worry about the opinion of others so much? Two years later and it would be that I should never use age, fitness, qualifications or any other self-limiting belief as a reason to avoid trying something new or different.

The 17-year-old me would provide counsel to always appear confident even if you're not, as it adds credibility to what you say. If I could throw some advice back to him I would tell the same 17-year-old that a touch of humility here and there doesn't go amiss, but that's for another time! The 19-year-old version would be proud of the fact that I am writing this book and tell me that searching for my own meaning in turn helps others to do the same and I should strive to find the right balance between the two.

Who'd have thought it? There was me an hour ago rewinding the clock 35 years and wondering if there was any mileage in this chapter and I bet you were doing the same. The reality is that we can learn from all our experiences, our trials, tribulations and tantrums, and in our teenage years they came along in droves!

There seems to be an unwritten rule that you can only give advice to people younger than you, or at a push the same age. I remember as a youngster being put in what was referred to as 'my place' on many an occasion with the 'when I want your advice I'll ask for it' retort by those who were my elders and allegedly my betters. I think we've moved on past the 'seen and not heard' days now though when referring to the next generations, don't you? Thank goodness for that I say, as we'd be missing out on some great observations, opinions and different perspectives.

So don't deny yourself the advice of the younger you. What would they say about the way that you are currently living your life and what changes would they be advocating? What would they be advising you to stop, start and continue doing? What would they think of the decisions that you have made recently? Would they approve of the company you keep and the way that you spend your time? What might they think you're doing a little too much of, and what would they be giving you a pat on the back for?

Did you like yourself as a teenager? Were you more at ease with yourself as you entered those years or when you left them? There's a big difference between 12 and 20 so how would the two outliers compare you if they were having a conversation? Wow – two versions of you having a chat about you! This is getting confusing, but fun! Did you like yourself as a teenager and would that teenager like you?

Would they admire you? Would they look up to you? Would they want to be like you when you grow up? What would they require of you in order to be more admiring and respectful and what changes in your behaviour would result in you becoming a greater role model to them?

You weren't perfect way back then, none of us were, but you did your best. Think of all those experiences, the highs and lows, the spectacular successes and the epic failures. Do you look back and just cringe with embarrassment, or do you take time to reflect on what happened, what really happened, and consider how you might learn from the past, however distant, to build for the future? It's not too late to let that person who shared your body but not your experiences back into your world. Who knows, they might just have some useful advice for you before it's too late.

33. HOW ARE YOU BUILDING ON RECENT SUCCESSES?

Life is full of highs and lows, peaks and troughs, where success and failure co-exist and bash into one another blurring the lines in-between. The fact that they come and go with such great regularity can ensure that they often get lost as we march forward relentlessly in pursuit of the next task on our to-do list.

An ex-colleague of mine, Steve, had a simple mantra – 'you win or you learn' – and to be fair he learned more than most. It worked though, as it always made you think how you could learn from what you might initially have perceived as a failure. I didn't know it at the time but this philosophy was espoused by none other than Nelson Mandela too. When Thomas Edison invented the lightbulb he didn't adopt a 'right first time' approach, learning from every time he got it wrong before he finally saw light at the end of the tunnel and wherever else he chose to illuminate his new idea.

So let's not lose sight of what Steve, Nelson and Thomas espoused (an unlikely group it must be said) but at the same time let's not bury the 'wins' from that either/or scenario under the carpet. Instead of rushing after the scent of the next success, we should stop and reflect on what went well, and why, then consider how we can replicate it elsewhere and build on it.

What are some of your recent successes and how are you building on them? I bet right now that you're racking your brain searching for those belters – those whopping great big wins that changed your life and those around you, bringing your retirement date forward a decade and was on the verge of putting your picture on the front page of the local gazette. Well, can I suggest that you stop looking quite so hard or setting your stall quite so high and come down a peg or too like the rest of us mere mortals have to.

Think of what grew well in your garden last year, or why the recent presentation you delivered was so well received. What did you do differently to enable you to knock five seconds off your personal best or why did that cake you baked gain so many plaudits? Successes come in various shapes and sizes – stop thinking of other people's for a minute and focus closer to home, on yours.

As you consider what some of those recent successes were, ask yourself these four questions and they might provide you with some pointers. When did you receive some positive feedback regarding a piece of work that you carried out? When did someone acknowledge your contribution or pay you a compliment? When were you asked for your advice on something? When were you pleased with how something went? And if you're still struggling how about this one – who has said thank you to you in the last hour, day, or week?

I have a book on my shelf that tells me where all the old phrases used in the English language come from, and I've just researched one that springs to mind as I write this: 'strike while the iron is hot'. I've never really considered myself to be a salesman in the traditional sense of the word, yet the reality is that we are all selling – our thoughts and ideas, seeking to influence others in some shape or form. In my work, the concept of cold calling isn't something that I'm particularly comfortable doing and the good news is that I haven't really had to. That's not a glib boast, it's just that my approach to winning more business is simple: when a piece of work goes well, I stay in touch with the happy customer. I ask them how else I can help them and who else I should be speaking to, aiming to avoid the one-hit wonder approach to business. Or, I'm hitting a piece of hot metal with a mallet before it cools while it is still hot enough to be shaped – otherwise known as striking while the iron is hot. Who or what do you need to seek to influence before it's too late? Let's avoid today's successes being tomorrow's fish and chips wrapper.

I'm going to let you into a secret. This isn't the first book that I've started writing but it will be the first one that gets published. I wrote 70,000 words that looked back on my relationships and experiences of life with a view to cajoling the reader to do the same, and in doing so empowering them to consider how they can learn from the past to build for the future. It was an incredibly cathartic experience that took up a great deal of my time and my heart. And then I just stopped, and the longer I stopped the harder it was to carry on. I was experiencing great success yet I didn't build on it – I should have seen it through to completion. The good news is that this book has superseded it and I much prefer both the subject and content of this current offering, but it's still a bit of a waste whichever way you look at it.

What projects have you started then pressed the pause button? What do you need to crack on with to ensure that you achieve the successes that would come your way if you were to proceed? Set yourself milestones and celebrate every time you reach them, happy in the knowledge that you are closer to reaching your ultimate goal as a result. Build on your successes however small they might seem. So how are you building on your recent successes? Who are you speaking to, emailing or generally keeping in contact with? Who should you be asking for feedback, a reference or a case study from, providing written evidence of a job well done?

Einstein said, "The definition of insanity is doing the same thing over and over again and expecting different results." I fully agree

Albert, particularly if whatever you did didn't work. That would be folly. But if you've been successful at whatever it is that you're doing, you should stop, reflect and document what made it the success that it was so that you can repeat it 'over and over again', leading to the same positive results.

Anything else would be insanity. Wouldn't it?

34. WHERE MIGHT YOU NEED TO CHANGE YOUR ATTITUDE?

Attitude is one of those words that only ever seems to get trotted out when combined with a select few additional words. When used positively it describes just that – a 'positive mental attitude'. Yet when used in a less favourable manner people might be accused of having an 'attitude problem'. So which of those two attitudinal caps fits best on your head?

Where do you display the more attractive of the two – full of uplifting and forward thrusting thoughts? Or is PMA more likely to stand for Pretty Mediocre Attempt or Pessimistic Minded Approach? I bet you display it somewhere – we all have it in us however much it chooses to stay behind gloomier clouds for periods of time. But that's not really what this question is about; the focus here is on where you might need to challenge the attitude that you have and subsequently change it because it isn't really serving you that well.

Ever heard someone say 'I'm not going to bother saying anything in that meeting as it'll only be held against me'? In fact, never mind anyone else, have you ever said that? If you've not said it have you ever thought it? When it comes to attitude, *thinking* it and *saying* it are two of the same – both resulting in a behaviour and action that is likely to lead to an unproductive result. You hear these types of statements all the time, either in conversation or in your own head. Statements like 'what's the point?' or 'it'll never last' or how about 'we've tried that before'. You could call them defeatist, negative or cynical but the one common denominator in them is that they all suggest that a change in attitude might be required.

Granted, if you've just lit a match it is fair comment to say that 'it'll never last', and the fact that you have 'tried it before' may well be an indisputable comment, but if they are additions to your dialogue that are purely designed to block progress then you should challenge yourself, your thinking and your attitude.

So what is this thing we refer to as attitude? It's a combination of your emotions, beliefs and behaviours towards something or someone or an event that has occurred. Our experiences may well have shaped them but they are not set in stone. You can and, in the past, you have changed them. Think back on where you have done just that – where you changed your attitude and benefited as a result. And while you're reflecting on personal productive examples you might want to contemplate where adopting a similar approach would help you currently to ensure a bit more of the same.

I'm not proud to say this but when I was younger I used to have a negative attitude towards people on the streets who were asking for money. People, that's what they are, people who have fallen on hard times and have most likely made some poor choices along the way. They are where they are and the rest of us should think ourselves lucky that our lives haven't taken the same path. Yet in days gone by my perception was that they were beggars who made the streets look untidy, intimidating law-abiding folk as they spent other people's money on drink and drugs.

You see, I even knew their life story and I'd never even spoken to them. How often do you fill in the gaps without knowing all the facts? I needed to change my attitude. I'm embarrassed as I read that last paragraph. Don't get me wrong, fast forward to the present day and I'm not the patron saint of the homeless, but I do like to think that my whole emotions, beliefs and behaviours on the whole subject, the three components of the attitude trilogy, are far more acceptable to both me and the people in the doorways of the towns and cities around the world.

As I focus on the present day, I think I need to change my attitude to people who don't support the same football team as me! Don't you dare go telling me it's just a game, I'll have none of that nonsense thank you very much, but I really do need to start behaving like a man in his 50s every now and then. Panic not, I'm no hooligan, but my attitude to football rivalry probably doesn't show me in the best light. Change your attitude man – they share the same love of the beautiful game as you and a passion for their team, supporting them through thick and thin (whatever that means). There, I feel better already – my attitude problem in this instance is not irreparable.

It's time to be honest with yourself – see how many of these statements you can identify with that might suggest where you need to change your attitude. Once you have a view on a person or situation do you tend to refuse to change it? Do you tend to see the negative in people or are you generally suspicious as to their motives if they do something for you? Do you tend to have an 'I'm right you're wrong – end of story' mindset? Do you tend to opt for revenge rather than forgiveness? Do you tend to look for someone else to blame when things go wrong?

As you look at that meaty old set of statements you'll see that one word that appears in all five is 'tend'. It's pretty unlikely that one of them would always apply to you but what is your tendency? If one or more of them seemed a bit too close to home then you're beginning to shine some light on where you might need to change your attitude.

And if at this point you're thinking to yourself 'it's not me that needs to change my attitude, it's other people', then you just created statement number six; most people with an 'attitude problem' would be likely to have that response up their sleeve when considering statements one to five.

So whether it's a case of being more positive, accepting or forgiving, or less intransigent, intolerant or blaming, where and how might you need to change your attitude? I guarantee that in all six of those 'more or less' cases you'll feel better as a result – about you, about others and about whatever situation it relates to.

You can do it, no problem.

35. IF LAUGHTER REALLY IS THE BEST MEDICINE, WHERE COULD YOU GET MORE OF IT?

When was the last time you laughed so much that it hurt? As far as pain goes, I can't think of a more enjoyable way to experience it – that beautiful, uncontrollable, liberating bout of the giggles. OK, so it might hurt your sides a little, or you may feel the odd tweak in your tummy, but the good that it does you far outweighs the harm.

Don't take my word for it. Medical research tells us that there is a whole gamut of reasons why it is so beneficial to our mind, body and soul, so consider how many of these you could do with adding to your own personal medicine cupboard. How about relieving a bit of physical tension and relaxing your muscles? Or maybe you quite fancy an endorphin releaser, those things that help to create a sense of wellbeing? Would you like to set your blood flowing a bit more freely and in turn help to prevent a number of rather serious conditions?

And if that little lot still doesn't have you reaching for the joke book, it's even suggested that laughter can help us reduce some of our excess by chipping away at those hard to shift calories. Don't throw in your gym towel just yet though, we're talking 20 calories for every five minutes of laughter, but by my calculations that's over

5,000 calories if you went for a full day non-stop! That's a pretty eclectic set of remedies to add to your cabinet don't you think?

So are you getting enough? Don't use the opening lines of this chapter as the barometer though; it doesn't have to hurt, those moments are pretty rare occurrences for all of us, but what about those times when someone has said something, or done something, or you have watched something and the result was an involuntary bout of laughter? Who makes you laugh? What makes you laugh? When do you laugh? I also fully understand that some of us like a good dose of tomfoolery and high jinks more than others, so I am not trying to turn us all into a pack of imbecilic hyenas, more asking you to consider how a little extra might help you in more ways than you might previously have been aware of.

Comedy is really important to me and I ensure that I avoid going more than three months without watching a comedian live on stage. Of course I have my favourites and a genre that suits me; if we all liked the same ones I'd have difficulty obtaining tickets to Dave Gorman, Jack Dee or Ed Byrne while others played to empty houses. I always feel better for the experience, and by the look of the other faces in the audience as the curtain closes, I'm not alone. My TV planner at home has four distinct types of programmes: sport, dramas, documentaries, and last but not least, comedy. So whether watching live or in the comfort of my own living room I plan for laughter (because if they don't make me laugh I stop watching, replacing them for something or someone that will). Where are you scheduling these moments into your world?

Now let's put those people who get paid to make you laugh to one side and come a bit closer to home, looking at friends, family and colleagues who do a pretty good job of doing the same without costing you a penny. In my home laughter is probably the noise that occurs most, dog barking aside, and the two main inhabitants are both very happy with this situation. We make each other laugh and that feels good. When observing situations, we look to extrapolate the funny components out of them. My best buddies make me laugh with their quick wit, irreverent mimicking and bursts of daftness. When we are together the conversation will invariably be interspersed with a not insignificant amount of in-house banter. In my work, I have colleagues and customers alike who are incredibly good fun – they make me smile and they make me laugh.

I don't get everything right in life, far from it, but one thing that I have got right is that I am surrounded by people who make me do something that is massively high on my list of things to do day in day out – laugh. How important is it to you and who are you surrounding yourself with that instigates it in you? The chances are you will laugh more when you are in the company of others than you will when you're on your own. Whose company should you be spending more time in? What circles should you be elbowing your way into so that you can exercise your funny bone?

How often do you get told jokes and subsequently forget them as soon as the punchline has been delivered? If you're one of those people who says 'I never remember jokes' then get into the habit of writing a couple of words down somewhere immediately after hearing it that will serve to remind you of it. Always have one up your sleeve to share, because after all, who doesn't love a good joke?

Are you able to laugh at yourself? Are you able to spot the humour in a situation and then share that tale with others so it puts a smile on their face or turns into something more audible? I always say it takes an awful lot of confidence to appear so self-effacing. Laugh at yourself without putting yourself down and it becomes an attractive quality that others will enjoy. You're probably funnier than you might think you are. Life is funnier than it sometimes feels. And other people, well they're just hilarious, you just need to get your humour radar working properly.

As with many other subjects contained within the questions and pages of this book it's useful to make notes of how often something has occurred, and in this instance how often you have laughed over a period of time and what was it that made you laugh. Don't document it straight away, that might dilute the fun at that precise moment in time, but at the end of the day just spend a couple of minutes asking yourself the question 'what or who made me laugh today?'.

If you can't think of anything, then that is a wake-up call. A whole day without laughter seems a very long time to me. In fact, it's no laughing matter.

36. WHAT WORDS WOULD YOU LIKE PEOPLE TO USE TO DESCRIBE YOU THAT THEY ARE UNLIKELY TO AT THE MOMENT?

I had dinner with an old friend of mine a couple of nights ago and five minutes into having been reunited after an 11-month hiatus she suggested that I was acting a little 'frenetic'. And there was me trying to come across as measured, calm and grounded. I'd been rumbled again! Frenetic is not a word that I'm too keen to be labelled with to be honest; it all seems a little too 'off the rails' for my liking, but she has an unswerving ability to choose the right word at the right time and it didn't fail her on this occasion either. I'd had a busy day and was trying and failing to juggle many balls simultaneously, of which she was one.

The reality is that neither a close friend nor a stranger meeting me for the first time would attribute any of the three words on my wish list to me however much I would like them to. I am the storm after the calm, and the last time I was grounded was when my mother wouldn't let me out of the house when I was nine. Oh, and the doctor measures me every ten years just after he's plonked me on the scales as a part of my once a decade health check.

What words are people unlikely to select when describing you however much you might want them to? Let's try and keep it real here though. There is no magic wand so let's park the 'tall, dark and handsome' response for another question and focus on those words that you would like people to say, and if you really chose to you could add them to your repertoire. I could work at being calmer; a bit of Pilates here and a spot of meditation there would go some way to help me lose the 'frenetic' tag that people will often observe but not necessarily say.

Take a look at this random bunch of words and if we use two axes they will fit into one of four categories. Those that you would like people to say and those that you would prefer them not to — that's one axis. Then the other one identifies those that they are likely to say through to those that they are unlikely to say. Where would you place thoughtful, sincere, vibrant or focused? How about genuine, dynamic, determined or deep? Let's throw a few curve balls in there with aloof, dismissive, indiscreet and stubborn. Throw some of your own into the mix while we're at it and finally stir my original three into the pot for good luck.

So which of that little lot would you like them to say and they would? I'm going for vibrant, what about you? What would you not want them to say, and they wouldn't? That's aloof for me. Moving into the 'frenetic' zone for me here — what would you not like them to say that they would? Which leaves us with the original question, what would you like them to say that they wouldn't? I'd like people to say that I am sincere but recognise that some of my more visible behaviours might tend to dominate that desired but less instantaneously recognisable trait. Play that one at home and see what common themes emerge for you.

How might you go about moving the words in this graph that we've created, so that you and those that you interact with are aligned in their thinking? The best way to acquire a new behaviour is to act as if you have it, so what actions should you be taking to adopt those characteristics that you would like others to observe when in your company?

I've worked with psychometrics for many years, helping individuals understand their behaviour and the impact that it has on others and I love all that stuff. I'm constantly asking people these types of questions and am endlessly curious with regards to what makes us similar and different. It's not a nine to five type of job as you can imagine as people tend to pop up all over the place!

Several years ago I was having a coffee with my mother (that's twice she's been mentioned in this question – she'll be after a cut of the profits at this rate) and I posed her a question. "If you could describe your three children in one word what words would you choose?" After the initial reaction that suggested that she was thinking 'do you ever stop with this nonsense?' she provided the first two parts of the trilogy. Beginning with the eldest she described my sister as 'caring' before moving on to my brother who she referred to as 'sensitive'. As she considered her youngest child, that's me, she paused as if trying to articulate herself in the most accurate way. "If I had to describe you in one word it would be, er... arrogant." She looked quite pleased that she had nailed it and completed her unexpected Saturday morning assignment.

I wasn't quite so pleased. I wasn't frustrated with her and I wasn't dismissive of her response but it was not really what I wanted to hear. Come on Mum, how about loving, funny, driven, energetic, compassionate – get the bloody dictionary out and choose any one of the thousands of positive words at your disposal! At various stages in the intervening years she has clarified that she meant 'confident' but in her world they are the same thing. I'd have liked her to say confident but she didn't, and it left me considering the subtle but significant shift between the two. What small shift could you take that would make a big difference in the perceptions that people would have of you and the words that they would use to articulate them?

Right that's another one finished. I've no doubt that you thought that was a brilliant question and chapter. I'm off to complete the other 100 things on my to-do list in the next half hour. Arrogant and frenetic? Don't you dare!

37. WHAT SHOULD YOU FINISH THAT YOU HAVE STARTED?

If you've ever been fortunate to have visited Barcelona then you'll no doubt have seen its most famous attraction, the Sagrada Familia. Whilst the vast majority of us love it there is still an element of architectural Marmite about it – hated, adored but never ignored. For those less enthusiastic observers I wouldn't mind a euro for each one of them who has uttered the words 'it'll be all right once it's finished'. Honestly, some people are so impatient! It'll be done by 2026, or so they say. Not bad really when you consider that work commenced on Gaudi's masterpiece in 1882. The poor chap will have been dead for a century before his vision is finally realised.

Imagine that, hey? It would be a bit of an anti-climax if I found out that this book wouldn't be published until the next century, long after I'd popped my clogs. What are you in the middle of right now that you would quite like to get finished while you're still around to see it? What project did you start but then put on the back burner until a later date? What a shame when it was all going so well. That pond in the garden that you were digging or that cardigan you were knitting – what happened to them? How about that cost-saving project at work or that commitment to get fitter?

As I write this, things are starting to come back to me that I had actually forgotten about and the chances are that you will be the same. My bike got dusted down a few years back and I had all sorts of plans to head out on adventures, feeling the wind in my hair (on my bald head is not a phrase so allow me to pretend for a minute) and a healthy tightening of my leg muscles. I'm not quite sure where my bike is at the minute but I did enjoy both of the rides that I embarked on!

I work across a range of industries but the one that I tend to spend most time in is the pharmaceutical industry. In doing so I gain a good insight into some of the challenges that they are faced with, and one of the biggest that impacts them, and as a result all of us, is influencing people to complete a course of prescribed treatment. Take a look at the various creams and pills that occupy your medicine cabinet. My guess would be that a good percentage of them are half used – not full and not nearly empty but somewhere in-between. The doctor didn't say 'just get halfway and it should be all right to leave it there' but you self-regulated. I'm not being all self-righteous here, mine is the same (I've just taken a peek in the name of research). We're all at it – a bunch of Beethovens and Schuberts with our unfinished symphonies. Who is the beneficiary of such truncated actions? I'd suggest that it is unlikely to be you.

So why do we do it? Do we get bored, do we change our mind or does something else come along that's either more important, more urgent or more appealing? Let me go through those five scenarios and see if I can find a full set of my own to help bring them to life for you. Other work priorities were more important for me to focus on than the coaching programme that I was creating; going to physio to address my aching knee was more urgent than continuing my visits for sleep-inducing acupuncture; and walking was deemed more appealing than cycling. I got bored with wine making and I changed my mind about upgrading the garden shed.

You see, I've covered all five of the options that I suggest can press the pause button on whatever it was that you were previously doing, and I reckon that if you stop to think about it you'll be able to do the same too. As you do just that, consider if one of them is, on reflection, worth carrying on with. I've found the one for me: the coaching programme is something that I shouldn't allow to be shelved as all the original reasons for working on it still exist.

To be clear, I'm not suggesting that you need to finish everything that you start. I have hideous memories as a five-year-old of being forced by a gang of nuns (that's not the official noun) to eat mashed potato. It wasn't nice when it first entered my mouth and it was a good deal worse 70 minutes later when they finally aborted their lunchtime strategy. You have my full permission to put something to one side if it is no longer relevant, important, or in my ordeal's case, edible. What I'm really wanting you to consider are those experiences, projects or pastimes that you might have either forgotten about or neglected that still interest you and would still add value to you, yet add no value in their current unfinished state.

As I've been writing this chapter there is a song that I can't get out of my mind, and it transpires that it is from the musical *Seesaw* (which you may recall more than me). The line that keeps repeating itself is 'it's not where you start it's where you finish and you're gonna finish on top'. If you were to finish whatever it is that you have started how would you be better off? What could you do, say, use or enjoy that you can't as it currently stands? Right now you're neither at the start nor at the finish, it's like being at the motorway services on a car journey, and who really wants to stay there for longer than is necessary?

The reality is today there is just so much to occupy all of our time, so why not delay starting things rather than starting them but not finishing? We get immense pleasure from completing tasks and no little frustration when we don't, so allow yourself to feel that sense of achievement by starting less and finishing more.

Don't beat yourself up though, maybe we all bite off a bit more than we can chew. If only those nuns were aware of such points.

38. WHERE MIGHT HONESTY BE THE BEST POLICY?

How many lies have you told in the last week? I bet you weren't expecting such accusatory questions when you purchased this book, were you? But before you start going all defensive on me I'm not talking about those whoppers here that leave you either riddled with guilt or covering your tracks. I'm thinking more of the 'white' version, those that are told because they represent the easy option, saving you from upsetting someone or having to explain yourself with the effort it takes perceived to be greater than the benefit.

However, the question doesn't have to be restricted to the words that you articulated. When I was a young boy I found a pound note on the driveway of a neighbour's house in the street that I lived and played in. I had a choice and the choice that I made was to keep it, resulting in a growing sense of guilt that lasted what seemed like an eternity. This large green piece of paper ceased to become legal tender in the 80s yet I still recall this bout of dishonesty with clarity and alarm even if the fear of a custodial sentence (and a clip round the ear, 70s style) has reduced somewhat over the years.

As with all of us, there have been a few more bursts of dishonesty between then and now to accompany that childhood misdemeanour, but thankfully not so many that it caused me to consider the validity of me writing this chapter. Or am I being economical with the truth? Ah, that's another way of looking at this question – I mean there's lies, there's dishonesty and there's just not being completely truthful. Add that one to the mix too – whichever way you look at it the question remains the same: moving forward, where might a more honest approach to your words and actions be the best option?

Think of those closest to you – would a few home truths benefit those with whom you co-habit or would you prefer to leave that particular applecart as it is? Honesty is a value that many of us hold dear yet we don't always live by the same standards that we expect from others. Yet when delivered with a positive intent, to provide feedback, clarity or a way forward it can only adversely impact the recipient if it is left unsaid.

How many times have you muttered under your breath in a restaurant that the food on your plate wasn't quite as enjoyable as you were expecting, but when the waiter/waitress returned to see how you were getting along with your meal you replied 'fine thanks'. The poor chef hadn't got a clue that his efforts over a hot stove had been in vain. How often has someone uttered those words to you where there was only one answer that would suffice: 'how do I look?' ('does my bum look big in this?' can also be used as an example here if you prefer). Did you give them an honest answer or the response that they wanted to hear? Which one did you plump for, the easy option or the honest one?

As I said previously, sometimes those white lies don't do any harm, yet what about those occasions when they don't provide any help, so no one gains? Feedback, they say, is a gift and many businesses are now striving to create a culture of real-time feedback where both the acknowledging and the developmental variety are provided as close to the event as possible. There are many models out there that provide a framework for such disclosure to take place and one of my favourites belongs to my old employee, Insights. They use a simple D4 model to provide feedback where the stages each begin with the same letter. Can you guess which one?

The first D stands for Data – what actually took place, what was said, done or observed (as it actually happened). We then move on to Depth of Feeling where you consider how you felt as a result of what took place. It's important here to remember that no one can ever challenge how you feel, those feelings belong to you and you alone. Then we move to number three, Dramatic Interpretation – as a result of feeling that way how did you interpret the situation? Picture the scene: when you cooked a meal for someone but they said on arrival 'I've just eaten'; you may well have felt frustrated and your dramatic interpretation might be 'why do I bother?'. The final stage is what you want the other person to Do with the feedback – what action would you like them to take? Something like 'Can you let me know in advance of me preparing the meal if you know you are not going to want to eat?'.

Think of someone who you would like to give honest feedback to and follow that model through in your own head before delivering it; it should help you along your way and avoid that frustrating, festering feeling of wanting to provide some honest commentary but not delivering it.

Have you really said how you feel about the recent additions to your workload? Are those tiles on the kitchen floor really to your taste or are you just striving to keep the peace? What was stopping you from being honest in expressing your thoughts and feelings on these matters or the equivalents that are taking place in your world at the moment?

So, we've looked at this issue from different angles. There's my pound note example, where being dishonest is just wrong (think karma and all that). Then there's thinking one thing and saying another. Not quite as bad as the previous point but not very authentic all the same, and authenticity is recognised as being a pretty smart trait to have in your locker. Then finally there's the scenario where you keep your thoughts and opinions to yourself for a range of reasons. For all three of these the question remains the same: where would honesty be the best policy?

Because let's face it, it invariably is, and that's no word of a lie.

39. WHAT SHOULD YOU BE PLANNING FOR?

We've just booked a city break in Seville and I'm in my element. Few things excite me more than preparing for a short break, researching all the must-see destinations, architectural beauty and the nooks and crannies that make every place populated on this planet refreshingly unique. When it comes to holidays long and short, I am a planner. Is that a word that you would use to describe yourself? Few traits tend to split us in two more than this one with the vast majority of us responding to the question posed with 'it depends on what I am doing'.

So what could you or should you be planning for? How's that Will coming along? Or what are you expecting from your pension as it currently stands, and do you have any plans for your retirement in general, regardless as to whether you are closer to 17 than 70? These questions might seem like they are in the dim and distant future so let's bring it closer to the current time and think about when your family pay you a visit, your kids go back to school or, given that I haven't a clue when you're reading this, Christmas. Come to think of it, some people will start planning for that annual holiday before they have taken down the decorations. Ever noticed how many people are buying cards in the shops in those few days before New Year? We're all different I guess but that little shopping spree is not for me!

Now let's shift the focus slightly and consider goal setting. I absolutely love setting goals, large and small. In my previous company we used to set what Jim Collins in his book *Good to Great* called BHAGs – big hairy audacious goals, the ones that when people heard them they thought 'there's absolutely no way that we will get anywhere near that'. At which point you have two choices really: have a go or give up.

Goals and plans are merry bedfellows and as Brian Tracy, the training and development guru said, "A goal without a plan is just a dream." I'm all for a bit of dreaming, but I'm with him on this one. If you want to reach your goals, a plan can only increase your chances of achieving them, however big or hairy or audacious they might be. What goals have you recently set where a clearer, more structured and well thought out plan would increase your chances of saying 'I did it'?

I get to meet some pretty special people in my work, and spending time with a team in Germany recently, I sat next to a guy at dinner who was in his 60s. We engaged in small talk where we discussed our love of being outdoors. It began by me talking about walking my dog and enjoying it even more if we don't pass a single soul as it provides me with some much needed reflection time. This was the catalyst for him to explain how he has a similar feeling when he goes out for a run. A run was what he called it but not the type of run that you and I might embark on. He went out for 'ultra' runs that would last for several days, taking part in races where he climbed up to the top of mountains and back down again as part of the 100 miles that formed the race. "How on earth do you manage to do that?" I asked with astonishment, and his reply was as simple as it could be. "I plan for it," he said. "If you want to complete an ultra-run you have to be ultra-prepared."

Suffice to say, I was ultra-impressed. He explained how he started the planning stage more than six months in advance of his latest adventure, meticulously giving thought to how long, how steep and how often he should be donning his trainers for a jog. Those five Ps that we've all heard about (or six if you prefer the slightly elongated and slightly less polite version) were at the forefront of his mind and enabled him to achieve his goal. Where might proper planning and preparation help you prevent poor performance?

What are those events that bring out the planner in you in the way that a few days away with family does for me and a few days running does for my dinner companion? Now we've given ourselves a pat on the back we need to consider where else that quality could or should be put to good use. After all, let's face it, who doesn't enjoy a holiday? So I'm probably not the only one who gives it consideration before embarking on such a journey. Whether it be deciding what you're going to wear or where you're going to visit, it's a feel-good experience. The same cannot be said for death. Well that's stopped us all in our tracks, hasn't it just?!

How much information do you personally have that, if you were to head upstairs, would be no use to anyone as they have no access to it? In the Jones household, information about the bills that are paid, the arrangements with all the utility companies and the accounts that hold varying amounts of money for different reasons is known by one person and one person alone. Guess what – it ain't me! This obviously could prove to be a challenge if that one person who holds the knowledge heads onwards and upwards with all that information safely tucked in their back pocket, so plans needed to be in place in order to avert that danger. Who knows what in your household, and who would benefit from knowing just a little bit more?

There's a Chinese proverb (if ever in doubt as to a proverb's origin we do tend to attribute it to the Chinese) that poses the question: when is the best time to plant a tree? Before you start delving too deep into the merits of March versus April, the answer is

20 years ago and the second best time is now. None of us actually like thinking about such eventualities do we (dying that is, not tree planting) yet if we don't do it now, when are we going to do it? What should you be planning for before it's too late? What seeds do you need to be planting whether you have an orchard in your back garden or not?

A word that people often use to describe my delivery style is spontaneous and I smile when I hear it. I smile because I know how much planning I put into my sessions that enables me to appear as such. When delivering presentation skills training, one of my key messages to my participants is 'it takes an awful lot of preparation and planning to appear so spontaneous'. You might have no need to improve your presentation skills and you might not have a desire to appear so spontaneous, so complete that sentence in your own way. 'It takes an awful lot of preparation and planning to appear so…'. So what? No rush, I'm off into the garden to plant a tree. Come back to me any time in the next 20 years.

40. WHERE COULD YOU DEMONSTRATE A LITTLE MORE TEAMWORK?

If you cast your mind back to all the interviews that you've ever attended the chances are that you will have been asked on more than one occasion 'are you a team player?' or words to that effect. What did you answer? As far as the questions in this book go it's in line to win an award in the 'no-brainer' category because if you wanted the job that you applied for you would really only ever answer positively. There is indeed 'no I in team' but you'll find at least one in each word in 'obvious interview questions'. Yet I guess this question is their 'starter for ten', providing you with the opportunity to identify where, when, who with and what the end result was.

So we should all have some examples of this up our sleeve if we want to impress our potential employers. Or anyone else for that matter, as when it comes to attractive traits, being a team player is a pretty useful one to have in your locker. Consider those teams that you are a part of in various areas of your life and the likelihood is that you are a member of more of them than you might initially think.

Let's provide a definition of a team, identified by the pair of team-building gurus Thiagarajan and Parker to help you identify how many you are firmly ensconced in. It's the one that I use as

I help senior leadership teams determine if they actually are a team or merely a group: 'A group of people with a high degree of interdependence geared towards the achievement of a goal or the completion of a task'. So if you have a common goal, and need each other in order to achieve it, then you're a team.

So does your contribution help move towards that common goal or do you have an adverse impact? Would your fellow team members see you as a team player, working for the greater good or do they view you as a saboteur? Think about the team that you see yourself being most connected to and ask yourself these questions. Do you put the needs of the team before your own? Do you focus on the team's purpose, goals, objectives and priorities rather than just your own? Are you aware of how your piece of the team jigsaw fits in with the other pieces around you? Do you share your successes and learnings so others can benefit from hearing about them? What about the other way round: do you celebrate the successes of team members and are you there to support when things go awry?

There's some overlap with those five questions, but as I always used to say when I was reluctantly wallpapering, a bit of overlap means there's no gaps. How did you show up in that last paragraph – are you a shining example of what a team player should look like, the one that all interviewers are looking for in amongst a field of team player wannabes? Or did one or more of those questions prick your conscience, helping you to recognise where a greater display of teamwork on your part could benefit the collective rather than the individual?

It's not just in your career though where these questions require thought and where this most valued of qualities is sought. Take a look closer to home and consider the role you play in the family and view yourself as a piece of that domestic puzzle that we referred to earlier. How is that collective sense of identity and purpose showing up, that sense of unity that brings you together and stands you apart? Then, after that emotive reflection, you can consider those social, sporting and spiritual circles that you might mix in and ask yourself the same.

It's reassuring for all of us to have a 'STAR' ready to share to demonstrate our teamwork credentials – where a Situation led to a Task that required an Action that produced a Result. Whether you're back on the interview circuit or not it's a useful reminder that we have it within us to do it. But what can you think of right here right now that would benefit from you taking a different course of action to achieve a more team-centric result? Who should you be talking to, collaborating and partnering with or aligning your priorities with that you aren't currently?

An investment bank that I was working with recently was striving to move towards a more team-centric approach. As a part of the initial solution I incorporated what I refer to as an A-Z exercise, where small teams had to identify attributes of an effective team, one for each of the 26 letters of the alphabet. Of course some letters are easier to complete than others, not all teams would benefit from a xylophone, but more often than not the lists of positive team qualities are completed. On this occasion the four sub-teams shared their responses with each other in order to identify the common themes that emerged.

As one team presented their flip chart to their colleagues they were met with approval until they progressed to the letter H. It was at that point that they stated that one quality of an effective team is harmony. It was as though someone had let a stink bomb off (and if you don't know what one of them is you obviously went to a different school from me). One particular guy was most affected, giving the appearance of the proverbial bulldog chewing a wasp. "Harmony?" he questioned with disdain. "What's that got to do with teamwork?", his face still riddled with a combination of mocking and shocking disbelief.

That one cameo appearance by the dissenter enabled the team to gain clarity on its challenges when it came to building a team ethos. There's no one right or wrong answer to what each letter should stand for, but harmony is surely more right than wrong. The 'every man and woman for themselves' approach that was previously deployed in this company needed to change, and quickly, with more harmony being one of the ingredients in the recipe.

What words would you dismiss if you were to conduct this exercise with your team? The next phase of the exercise was for individuals to walk the flip charts in the room, identifying which of the attributes they personally added to and detracted from within the team. Imagine you were doing the same − what words would you identify with in a list that provides the answer to 'what constitutes an effective team?' and which ones do you detract from?

So whether you need to be a little more ambitious, brave and challenging, or amiable, buoyant and caring, what steps can you take to display more teamwork than you currently do? It's as easy as ABC.

41. WHERE SHOULD YOU BE PRACTISING WHAT YOU PREACH?

How many times have you asked or told someone to do something that you don't do yourself? Even if you haven't actually mentioned anything to that person directly, have you ever commented to someone else on what the behaviour or action should be from the third party? Go on, hands up! You're not alone I can assure you.

Now cast your mind back to your childhood. Were you ever on the receiving end of that most irritating of comments by a fractious parent 'do as I say not as I do'? It's not something you'll find in the best-selling 'how to be a wonderful parent' book yet it's a well-used statement to put an end to any challenge from the younger of the two warring factions.

Fast forward to the present day and is that an approach that you take with your children, partner, friends, colleagues or those that report into you? You see, it's not the sole preserve of parents from yesteryear, it's rife in all aspects of our world and I want you to cut it out right this minute. I'll start next week. Or maybe I should practise what I preach and start this journey with you.

Have you ever seen negative aspects of behaviour in others when, if you stopped to analyse your own behaviour in more detail, you would find those same behaviours within? In the psychological world this is known as projection. Think about those behaviours that others exhibit and contemplate if you are guilty of displaying the very same. When finding fault in others and criticising them for the behaviour on display maybe we should practise what we preach by asking ourselves a question before coming forward with our show of discontent. 'Am I finding unacceptable in someone else something that either I find unacceptable in myself or others might find unacceptable in me?'

I was in a meeting recently with a bunch of people who knew each other well, a creative think tank designing new products to incorporate into solutions. It was my type of meeting, rich in dialogue and outcomes, with a healthy dose of banter thrown in for good measure. One of my colleagues had been on a roll for a good while, providing insight and ideas but was just taking a little bit more air space and longer to make his point than I would ordinarily have liked. As he left the room I made a passing comment, more in jest than in criticism.

As soon as the words had left my mouth all four of the remaining participants laughed out a lot louder than I thought my comment deserved. All I said was, "He doesn't know when to shut up." The reason for the hysterics was nothing to do with the person who had temporarily left the meeting but everything to do with me and my resemblance to a pot referring to the absent kettle. If other people's ability to take more words than required to make their point is a source of frustration to me, then perhaps I need to review my own approach. Sometimes less might be more, in others and in myself.

I used to see a doctor many years ago and he was a great help to me when I was feeling low at the time of a break-up of a relationship. He listened to me, giving advice where required and ultimately prescribed me with a course of medication. It was a sad day when, six months later, I phoned to book an appointment with the same doctor on an altogether different issue, only to find out that he had taken his own life a few months earlier. How could a doctor, that person who appears to the rest of us to have an answer for everything, not be able to help himself?

At the same surgery I was asked to make an appointment with the nurse a few years later when my blood pressure was showing signs of being higher than desired. She provided me with a plethora of ideas as to how I could reduce my weight, which was useful yet I struggled to get past the fact that she was the largest nurse I'd ever met. I do not wish to be rude, personal or flippant but my mind was thinking 'have you read this yourself?'. When I worked in a bank I was amazed how many people were in debt, you hear about police officers breaking the law and members of the clergy committing heinous crimes. What do you do in your professional life and what have you done to demonstrate that you practise what you preach?

There are exceptions to every rule of course. For instance, when a midwife says 'push' she doesn't have to push herself. When you have a job like mine that helps people to cultivate more productive, harmonious and synergistic relationships, you put yourself up there to be scrutinised. I'm constantly reminded by closest loved ones that 'if you preach it, you need to practise it'. What are you preaching? If you're not keen on the word preach, how about what are you suggesting, telling or asking people to do that you are not doing yourself?

Allow me to introduce you to Charles Spurgeon. He was a Baptist preacher in the 19th century and was bestowed the lofty title 'prince of preachers', so as you might expect from one with such a title he was good for the odd quote or two. He said, "Sincerity makes the very least person to be of more value than the most talented hypocrite." The idea of someone being labelled as 'the very least person' doesn't sit too comfortably with me but, that small point aside, he's introduced an emotive word into proceedings. We started this chapter with projection and we've ended it with hypocrisy, and if we weren't really keen on being a serial projector we most definitely don't want to be seen as a hypocrite.

So, what do you need to stop, start or continue doing in order to move to the sincere end of the spectrum? Now all you need to do is ensure that you implement your action plan before telling anyone else to do the same.

42. WHERE DOES YOUR VOICE NEED TO BE HEARD MORE?

If you're reading this book the likelihood is that you are residing in one of the countries in the world that has freedom of speech. As a result, you have the right to voice your opinion publicly without fear of either censorship or punishment. You might think 'well so what?' and if you lived in one of the many places on the planet where this is not the case you wouldn't be thinking that. In essence, we take it for granted having never known any different, with the exception of being chastised by our parents in our formative years if what came out of our mouths wasn't met with their approval.

So, given that we're fortunate, within reason, to be able to say what we want when we want to who we want, where should you be making more effective use of the freedom at your disposal?

A few pages ago I asked you if you had ever been in a restaurant and felt unhappy with either the food that was on your plate or the service that accompanied it yet, when asked 'is everything ok with your meal?' you smiled and replied 'yes, lovely thanks'. What's that all about? Now I know some of you don't want to make 'a scene' but you had the chance and you chose not to say anything. Well you said something but not what you actually thought. It didn't help anyone really but hey, there was no 'scene' so all was good.

But imagine that scenario playing out in other aspects of your world, and you might not need to imagine too long and hard as it may well do just that. Consider your interactions and conversations over the last couple of weeks with those you know well and those strangers who you either met for the first time or who came and went never to be encountered again. Was there alignment between what you thought and what you said or did you keep it all in, creating the possibility of festering resentment or the feeling of a missed opportunity?

The reasons why people don't speak up to make public what they were thinking slot into four different categories. Firstly, they don't want to be the focus of attention and prefer to keep their view private. Secondly, they might either be lacking in confidence and conviction or concerned about being publicly embarrassed in any way. Then there's concern for how their words might be received and any subsequent repercussions or how others might perceive them for having said what they said. Finally, they might not think it is worth it and doubt that it would add value in any way to the conversation or situation.

All of these might be valid at any moment in time of course, so don't dismiss them as options just yet but consider if any of them resonate with a recent experience that you have encountered. Who might have missed out from hearing your thoughts or feelings in that moment in time? Did you suffer in silence as a result of keeping quiet? Were you left thinking 'I should have said…'?

If in doubt as to the appropriateness of making your voice heard, it's worth reflecting on the words of Buddha or Rumi or Shirdi Sai Baba or a whole range of people it has been attributed to. "Before you speak, let your words pass through three gates. At the first gate ask yourself 'Is it true?' At the second gate ask 'Is it necessary?' At the third gate ask 'Is it kind?'" So if the words are true (either your truth or a fair representation of the situation), necessary and kind then the world benefits from them being aired. You might think, therefore, that we can't criticise because that's not being kind yet I see kind in this situation being more of a positive intention. I can't change it though as it wasn't my quote, it was everyone else's!

Those with a more introverted preference are more likely to keep their thoughts, feelings, emotions and opinions to themselves. For those of us with a different preference, making ourselves heard is less of an issue because, as extroverts, we 'speak to think'. I used to co-facilitate a workshop called Successful Work Relationships and it was on here some 23 years ago that I received a piece of feedback that has stayed with me ever since.

One of my recent roles has required me to determine which facilitator should deliver which programme, and when it warranted two people I would purposely look for two facilitators with opposing and complementary styles. The same wasn't the case back in the 90s and on the course in question I shared the workshop with another extrovert. Let's call him John. After the course had finished we collected the dreaded course appraisal forms and one of them contained the following comment: 'Both John and Mike seemed to like the sound of their own voices, the difference was that we also liked the sound of Mike's!'.

If that had been the other way round I probably wouldn't be doing what I am doing now as I would have been traumatised by the experience. Poor John and lucky me, on another day the boot could have been on a different facilitator's foot. It was a lesson for us: if you really want your voice to be heard in the most effective way you might want to think about removing some of the clutter that surrounds it, ensuring that your headline news isn't lost amongst the gossip pages and classified ads.

The participant who provided the feedback was certainly 'heard' with his written words. Little did he know that fast forward a few years and the written word would enable our voices to be heard quite so loudly with the advent of social media. Few things deflate me more than reading the nasty comments of anonymous keyboard warriors (not in my direction you understand) and I suspect that they aren't quite so concerned which gates they pass through. Still, they're not reading this book and you are, so how could you apply that same key message from earlier in your written 'voice'?

So who needs to hear your voice right now? Who needs to hear your thoughts on that project, product or customer in the workplace? Are you giving as much as you receive on online forums where other people's opinions help inform your decisions? Who might need you to stick up for them, a case for the defence to balance the attack that is coming from other directions? What breakthrough ideas do you have that are adding no value by not being shared but could make a difference to someone or something sooner than you might think if you put them out there?

We all have a voice and we all need to use it. If you're not, you need to have a word with yourself, out loud.

43. WHERE MIGHT YOU NEED TO RAISE THE BAR A LITTLE HIGHER?

Play along with me at home now please. Put your right arm in the air and stretch it as high as it can possibly go. Good, thank you. Now stretch it a little bit more. What happened there then? I reckon that you found a little bit more from somewhere even though the first request was to stretch it as high as you could. So where did that little extra come from? Fancy you keeping it in reserve just in case an additional request came along.

How does that little physical exertion that got this chapter off to an interactive start compare to your world at the moment? Where are you currently not quite stretching as far as you might, either through choice or through not actually realising that you were capable of upping the ante in any way? The obvious place to look is in your health and fitness regime. Yes, let's call it a regime for the moment even though it may be more akin to a requiem.

My gym partner is a brute. She makes me do all sorts of hideous bursts of exercise under the umbrella of 'high intensity training'. She's a beast, and she's my daughter! Apparently she adds these short, sharp impromptu sessions into our gym visits to raise the bar, taking her dear dad to a level that he didn't think was possible. Don't get me wrong, there is a long way to go but my gym visits are more beneficial with this masochist by my side.

Do you reduce the speed on the treadmill or truncate your 30-minute session on the bike because you are at breaking point or do you just get a bit bored, biting off more than you thought you could chew? Crikey, now we're all contemplating the quality and quantity of what we tuck away – does that change in direction provide you with any clues as to where your bar (or biscuit tin) needs to be raised higher?

Michelangelo said, "The greatest danger for most of us is not that our aim is too high and we miss it, but that it is too low and we reach it." So what would you prefer, the aim high and miss combo or the aim low and reach? Having watched England miss a fair few penalties in important football games over the years, the latter has its appeal, but I don't think Michelangelo was referring to the World Cup. Are targets there to be reached or smashed? Think about that for a moment and consider a target that you are aiming for. Who set the target, was it you or someone else? Now what are you aiming for – the target or beyond?

I was privileged recently to share a stage on the Gold Coast, Australia with one of their own, a famous actor in those parts named Samuel Johnson. He was opening a conference for a giant pharmaceutical company and was positioned on the agenda as an 'inspirational speaker'. Having heard his story, I think they chose those two words well.

In 2003 Sam unicycled from Melbourne to Sydney to raise money for a children's charity, which you might think was enough material to qualify for the 'inspirational speaker' tag. Look on a map and you'll find that they are quite close, then you realise it's Australia we are talking about and 'quite close' means 900 kilometres apart. It takes nine hours to drive and four wheels tend to go quicker than one. But that was a mere canapé compared to his main course. His emotional story revealed how his sister was dying of cancer, so in 2013 he decided to raise money for her charity by unicycling

15,000 kilometres around Australia. His bar was already high ten years previously yet he had just raised it a whole lot higher.

In completing such an unbelievable feat, he raised over $1.5 million yet he was still intent on setting his sights higher. When his sister was dying he promised her that he would increase that to $10 million and as he took to the stage in Surfer's Paradise he was closing in on that figure. Just wow!

I came away from his session reflecting on my own goals and targets and wondered if they were just a bit too attainable and if I should be aiming higher, even if, as Michelangelo said, I might miss. Are the targets that you set high enough or should you be stretching yourself just that little bit more? And if so, where? I can only begin to imagine the combination of pain, pleasure, purpose and pride that Sam felt during his journey, but what I do know is that as he bounced around on stage in his charismatic style, one of them was no longer accompanying him. Can you guess which one? As far as a gang of Ps go, three of them are more appealing than the other yet what do they say? No pain no gain – or maybe we should amend that to 'no pain, no pleasure, purpose and pride'. Which of those four are you experiencing right now in your world and what would you need to do to increase the amounts?

The reality is that we are all far more capable of achieving more than we do if we put our minds and hearts to it. We've all heard of the comfort zone and we all spend a good portion of our time in it. That's not wrong as we need to regroup, recharge and take stock in the same way that we need to eat, drink and sleep. But if we spend all of our time in the comfort zone then we should think about renaming it to the unambitious zone, or the boring zone or (ouch) the lazy zone. Try not to stay in there for longer than you need to. Go on, hands up, who thinks they spend too much time in that zone, whatever we choose to call it? Now put it as high as it can go.

44. IF PRACTICE MAKES PERFECT WHAT DO YOU NEED TO PRACTISE?

I used to work with a glass half empty character and he had a plaque erected behind his desk that made people aware of his take on a well-known philosophy, designed to ensure that people thought twice before opening their mouths in his direction as they entered his office. It read 'A problem shared is a problem doubled' and it did the trick, the miserable git.

There's always more than one way of looking at everything – do too many cooks spoil the broth or do many hands make light work? If at first you don't succeed... know how that one ends? Originally it was the first half of the motivational mantra that ended with 'try try again'. It seems though that my 'problem doubled' guy was not alone as this happy ending has been replaced with the blunter 'give up' version by those 'it's funny to be cynical' kind. Well you little devils, fancy ruining such a fine philosophy.

So let me try and be the case for the defence of the 'try try again' approach. Keep going, you'll get there in the end! That not enough? OK, let's have a think about it for a minute. What were you once not very good at but now you are? The chances are that you didn't just go to bed one night, then wake up and everything had changed. You didn't just have one driving lesson before you zoomed down the motorway, or become bilingual after an hour in the company of the French teacher. The armbands weren't removed just prior to swimming your first mile, and that first presentation you delivered probably wasn't presented with quite the same aplomb as the last one.

Practice does make perfect. So for that matter does dedication, hard work, determination and sacrifice but that wouldn't make for quite the same snappy question really. Think for a minute where your own actions and commitment have proved this mantra and then think for another minute where it would help you in your current endeavours.

Recently my middle daughter, Ash, went on her first ever skiing trip with school, and as every proud parent would, I sent her on her way with a hug and a pep talk, slightly nervous as to whether she would be OK given that she had never done it before. The slight difference being that my daughter was one of the four teachers on the trip and the only one that was about to venture on to the slopes for the first time. She would be responsible for the fearless teenagers, while simultaneously attempting to allay all the same fears in herself that they seemed to be missing.

Our conversation stuck to the WhatsApp kind – short, snappy and often – and the messages across the week make my point far better than I can. Day one on the snow and the first message appeared stating 'I am very nervous'. To be expected I guess, as was 'I have fallen over a LOT'. Slightly more troubling, given her role as chaperone was 'I have skied into the children and knocked them over'. Still, all part of the fun and games of a school trip. Two days later I was saddened to receive 'I've had a bit of a cry' – I mean what parent wants to receive such emotion from their 26-year-old, particularly when one normally so strong and certain continues 'I had a confidence crisis when we did a really long steep slope'.

By this point I was concerned that the week was going downhill fast but not in the way that we had envisaged, but I shouldn't have worried. As the days passed the messages slowly but surely turned the corner, and so did she with the appropriate bending of the knees. The next message was altogether more uplifting – 'having an amazing time!' and the day after she proclaimed that she had 'undergone a big mental challenge this week' and that she had felt 'strengthened because of it'. I was loving this. Practice makes perfect on the slopes in the same way as it does in the office, in the home or in the pursuit of excellence. Day five and she told me 'apparently I have 'style' according to the pupils'. Wow she's now got a swagger on the piste! These are the same kids that she nearly scarred for life a few days earlier. She had persevered, shown determination, not lost sight of the goal and learned from her mistakes. She might not be ready for the winter Olympics but her regular practice was ensuring regular progress.

What do you need to be practising more to ensure your progress in the quest for something a bit closer to perfection? We've all heard of sports stars who were obsessed with their art, repeating the same technique over and over again in their desire to reach the top of their game. For the rest of us mere mortals that might not be quite so practical. The hours spent fine-tuning his free kick strategy was time well spent for Ronaldo but you might not have a spare three hours to do the same in whatever subject you're trying to burst the back of the net in. So what does it look like for you, this practice malarkey? What should you be doing, when should you be doing it and who should you be doing it with? It doesn't have to eat up every hour that God sends, but let's face it, how else are you going to improve?

When I look back on the first ever training course that I delivered back in 1991 it was pretty average. It was scripted, stilted and I spilt water all over my slides such was the extent of my nerves. I don't profess to being the world's best nearly 30 years later but I sure am a whole lot more confident and competent than I was. That alliterative pair often work in tandem with an increase in one leading to an increase in the other. What would you like to be more confident in and competent at, and is the amount of practice that you are doing moving you in the right direction?

If not then contact me – a problem shared is a problem halved, whatever old grumpy chops might have thought.

45. WHAT ADDITIONS TO YOUR DAILY ROUTINE WOULD MAKE YOU FEEL BETTER?

I went to my doctor a couple of years ago about a minor issue, and as usual I was in a bit of a rush. While there he glanced at my history on his screen and reminded me that I had just passed the half a century. His reason for doing this wasn't to congratulate me on my achievement for getting so far, it was to suggest that a few checks were in order in the same way you would do with a car that was showing a few signs of wear and tear. In my quest to be in and out in the quickest time possible, I said, "You probably don't need to, doctor, I'm not ill." His reply was one that I have referred to on countless occasions since: "You don't have to be ill to get better." There, I've used it again.

So let's work on the premise that you're not ill but you could still do with feeling just that little bit better. What could you do that you are not currently doing that could help you on your way? Tesco have reminded us for years that 'every little helps' so let's take their marketing gurus' word for it and apply that philosophy to our day.

I've got a sore knee primarily due to the fact that I used to go around kicking people on a football pitch for many years. It's uncomfortable more than painful and something that I just live with, nagging away as I embark on long walks, and often the subject of my moans and groans at the end of a physically taxing day.

The aforementioned doctor didn't seem too concerned and merely reminded me of my age when I said that my knee was creaking. He knew how to get my dander up playing the age card, something that we commit to never doing in our house, so I cursed under my breath and booked an appointment to see a physio.

He seemed far more interested and optimistic and took me through a range of exercises that would ensure that my mobility would be around for a few years yet. Twice a day for ten minutes I go through a series of stretches and I feel better as a result. I'm a bit late to the party on this one but stretching is good for you! Whether it's yoga or yawning, it's a good addition to a daily routine. What could you do for ten or 20 minutes a day that would be of benefit to you?

It doesn't even need to be that long. It only takes a few minutes to make that late night cup of hot chocolate, to read a poem, to listen to a favourite song or to write in a journal. Ever been too busy to read a bed-time story? And by the way, that doesn't just have to be for the under tens. I have a friend who reads to his wife for 30 minutes every night before they turn off the light. What a beautiful part of their routine as they focus on living happily ever after. We're all different however so that might not be your thing, but if not that, then what?

In amongst this book that comprises hundreds of questions, one of the chapter heading questions is 'What are you looking forward to most right now?'. This is a question that I ask myself with great regularity and the answer can be events and experiences that are in the dim and distant future. A more immediate question is 'what are you looking forward to about tomorrow?'. Who are you seeing, what are you doing, why are you doing it, and where are you doing it?

Not every day contains enough material to be made into a blockbuster film but more days than not are populated with a combination of moments that are worth looking forward to – whether they occur every day, every week or are unique. I'm not here to answer the question for you but I do suggest that asking yourself and subsequently answering what are you looking forward to tomorrow would be a positive addition to your daily routine just before or after you've turned off the light and said goodnight to the world (or finished reading that story to the person next to you).

How often do you find that the people you co-habit with are staring into their phones, communicating with an outside world at the expense of the people who share the same postcode? Far be it from me to change the culture of a generation, but if you could have 15 minutes of undivided attention from all the inhabitants of your home what would you say or do in that quarter of an hour? How about one of these questions to throw into the mix, leaving whoever has an answer to share and whoever doesn't to listen. What's on your mind? What have you learned today? What made you smile? What's troubling you? What are you excited about? Try it – phones away, television off, magazines down. The strongest families talk to each other and with each other, not just at each other. Fancy a bit more of that around your table?

Whether it's a walk or a run, a newspaper or a snooze, what could you add to your daily routine that would make you feel more relaxed, more energised, more connected or more informed? Whichever of those four sounds most appealing to you it would lead to the same end result – feeling just that little bit better. Think of those moments that occur every day in your life. There's probably too many to count, whether it be cleaning your teeth, walking your dog, boiling the kettle or looking at Facebook, most of us are comforted by some kind of routine – those elements of familiarity that make our day that bit more predictable in an unpredictable world. What could you add to that list that if you were to do it every day would quickly become routine – a positive, productive, enjoyable value-adding addition to your routine?

If you're reading this and you're not feeling well, then get well soon. If you're reading this and you feel absolutely fine, then get better soon. You don't have to be ill to get better. Thanks Doc.

46. WHAT IS YOUR PURPOSE?

Why are you reading this book? Go on, what's your purpose? You won't offend me with your answer so ask yourself that question. Now think about what you've either done or will be doing today – what's the purpose behind everything else that you have or will encounter? Sometimes the answer is pretty simple, and other times, like many of the questions in this book, an immediate answer isn't forthcoming. That doesn't mean you should ignore it though, because crack this one and everything that you do makes perfect sense.

Let me give you my answer to that question in eight words: to make people smile, laugh, think and act. If you were to strive to articulate yours in a similarly pithy manner what would it be? The good news is that you're not restricted to so few words in your quest to say why you do what you do, so take as many as you'd like.

When I set up my own company nearly five years ago the most cathartic element of the process was creating the website. The reality is it doesn't generate much business but it cajoled me into writing down what I did but more importantly why I did it – in essence the purpose of the business. Because it was my business it quickly became apparent to me that the company purpose and my own purpose were inextricably linked, and that felt good.

Let me ask you a series of questions that are all connected in some way that might help you to gain greater clarity on what your purpose is. Why do you go to work? Why do you get up in the morning? What difference do you want to make? What are you in pursuit of? What are you doing when you lose all track of time? Five questions that you may well not have an answer to – yet. You won't be alone because even though everything that we accomplish in life, however big or small, has a purpose, we often don't stop to consider what that purpose is.

The chances are that your first answer to some or all of these questions will fit into either the superficial or flippant category, and that's OK! But when considering why you get up, move beyond the 'because he wants to make the bed' answer, and when reflecting on why you go to work, dig a few spadefuls deeper than the 'to earn money' response. There's more to it than that.

Simon Sinek, one of the most gifted of thought leaders, suggests that we should begin with the 'why' and not the 'what' when considering our reason for doing what we do. I design and deliver learning solutions – that's what I do. Why do I do it? Because I want to make people think and act – do something with the learning. In addition to that I want to make them smile and laugh along the way.

So park the 'what' for a moment and consider why you do what you do – the reason for you going to work, and potentially the reason why you get up in the morning. Hopefully it's a part of the reason why you get up – add to that list and it should help you realise how invaluable you are to the world! The world that you are a fully-fledged member of, so what difference do you want to make in it?

I was delayed on a recent trip through London due to a demonstration by climate protestors. In their quest to highlight the issue to the world they set about disrupting the movement of thousands of commuters. Now on reflection my considered view of these people is that they are making a brave and active stance against a catastrophic issue, and the history books are populated with examples of where positive change has only come about due to this course of action.

Yet on that day my first thought was 'how inconvenient… I hope it doesn't adversely impact my travel plans for the day' or words to that effect. I even at one point regressed to a 'they must have a lot of spare time on their hands' response, yet I much preferred my reflective view of how clear and committed they are to their purpose. What is your purpose and how committed are you to it? They are in pursuit of a more environmentally friendly and responsible world, so they can tick that question off the list of the five that I posed you a moment ago. Can you?

I consider myself to be lucky because there is so much about my work that I enjoy and I get paid to do what I am passionate about. I'm mindful that not everyone feels the same but there is one well-known story that I want you to consider and it's a story that has been doing the rounds for a good few years – over 300 of them in fact.

Three bricklayers were asked what they were doing one day as they were going about their job. The first replied, "I'm working – laying bricks." Makes sense I guess, that was after all exactly what he was doing. The other had a bit more of a spring in his step and shared, "I'm building a wall." Christopher Wren was the one who asked the question, and the third bricklayer proclaimed, "I'm building a beautiful cathedral." Between them Wren and the bricklayers were creating the St Paul's Cathedral that we know and love today.

The third bricklayer had clarity and pride in his purpose, and if this story that has grown a few arms and legs over the years is true, he went at a quicker pace as a result of it. Purpose and productivity are intrinsically linked. When you consider where your productivity is at its highest I guarantee that you have clarity on your purpose in that area.

If you find yourself running around after other people, big and small, for half your life there is a reason why you do it – what is it? If you seem to spend hour after hour in the gym, there's a method in your madness, and if you are burying your head in books, taking exam after exam, you know where you want it to lead don't you? When we're busy and on purpose we're productive. If we're busy and not 'on purpose' we can be resentful and I know which one of those two you prefer.

OK I'd best finish there, I need to be elsewhere sharpish – I hadn't realised what time it was as I was enjoying writing this chapter so much. Which reminds me of my fifth question – got an answer for that one yet?

47. WHO DO YOU NEED TO SPEAK TO THAT YOU'VE NOT SPOKEN TO FOR A WHILE AND HOW WILL IT HELP YOU?

As you look back on your career who have been your mentors — those people that you looked up to and learned from as you watched them go about their business? I met up with one of mine last year for the first time in over a decade and within the first couple of beers I was wondering why I had left it so long. We laughed, reminisced, shared stories, asked each other questions and listened to the answers that followed.

Duncan was my manager's manager for a period of three years over 25 years ago and I've subsequently met up with him again since as part of our agreement to not leave it for more than six months without a face to face catch up. Even though he is no longer above me in the management pecking order, in fact he's no longer working, I learned a whole host of new 'stuff' from him. Some of it was more useful than others but the time spent in his company was enjoyable and beneficial, sharing some sound business advice, insightful ideas for my book and informed opinion on issues that the world wasn't faced with when we worked together. Is there a Duncan that has played a part in your life whom you would benefit from speaking to?

Cast the net a bit wider and you might consider people from all areas of your life where a conversation might add a little value to your world. Who are those friends from days gone by that you would like to reconnect with? Good old Facebook provided me with a chance to reunite with a bunch of old mates from many years ago recently and, as with Duncan, we've agreed to stay connected in an age where there is no reason not to do so. Who are those friends who you lost contact with for whatever reason where a conversation or two would be of benefit? Let's face it, a good chat, the odd laugh and a chance to reminisce is a benefit, so you don't have to go looking too hard for the upsides of such an encounter.

I'm never quite sure where my work is going to come from, but before you start thinking that any success that comes my way must therefore be based firmly on luck more than judgment, I know why it's going to come my way and on what topics, but it's the people who I am never sure of. Some clients come and go fairly quickly in their quest for a one-hit wonder burst of development, and others stay for the long haul (and I must say I do prefer these type). Generally, the work comes to me without me having to go overtly looking for it, but there was a period a couple of years ago where I doubted myself and wondered whether this self-employment idea was such a good one.

So one week I decided to write down a list of some people who slotted into the question of this chapter – people who I knew but hadn't made any contact with for a good while. The results were immediate and, three years later, I haven't had to repeat the task since. A series of conversations and interactions led to a variety of projects coming my way which made me realise that we all have a network but often we are guilty of not making it work to our advantage.

It works both ways though, so if you want to receive you've got to give. If someone from my past, however recent or distant, asks to chat I never say no. A few have tried to sell me items or concepts that I didn't want or had no need for, but speak to them I did. So who is in your network that could help you in your quest to make progress?

So we've talked about making pals and making progress but what about adding another P to the mix – peace. Who have you not spoken to for a while because of a disagreement that you once had where, on reflection, it might be time to reach for the olive branch? And if you did how would you benefit? Life's too short to bear a grudge and it's too beautiful to deny ourselves the company and conversation of those that we are fond of.

The thought that life is too short will ring true for those who have lost a loved one and suffered the grief that only that kind of departure can bring. Yet we can gain great comfort from speaking to those who are no longer with us, so consider them for a moment. What do you want to speak to them about, what news do you want to share or what advice would they give you should you ask for it? We don't always need to hear someone to answer back to gain benefit from talking to them. Yes, a conversation is a two-way process but it doesn't have to comprise two equal parts.

As you read this chapter, hopefully a few people would have crossed your mind, and fingers crossed, you might reach out to a few of them as a result. They're probably the friendly ones, the ones who will greet your voice with warmth and only an extensive to-do list or apathy is blocking your path. But what about the others, those you know you should be speaking to but you are putting off making that connection? You had a fall-out or maybe too much water has passed under the bridge that connected you. Just ask yourself would there be any benefit in having a conversation, and if the answer is yes then what is stopping you?

I'm glad I reconnected with some old friends from my teenage years and it's great to combine our old 'greatest hits' tales with some of the more recent tracks from our playlist. We're back in each other's lives. It's also good to have that wise old owl Duncan around with his unique combination of intellect and irreverence. I've made a connection with the past that I thought had gone. Where could you do the same?

48. WHAT OR WHO SHOULD YOU BE SURROUNDING YOURSELF WITH?

When I was a youngster my mum always had an opinion on the friendship circles that I mixed in and was quick to let me know who she approved of and who she didn't. Sometimes based on evidence and other times based on her instinct or perception, she would tell me who I should and shouldn't be hanging around with. She was a great fan of the more wholesome character, the one who in her opinion came from the right kind of family and who lived on the right side of town.

Now I'm a firm believer that in the sanitised world we have come to live in it's healthy for our kids to be exposed to a few mucky tables, building up immune systems and a bank of experiences along the way. Looking back I'm not convinced that my mum was!

So I'm not going to revert to her approach here but I am going to ask you, in a non-punitive manner you understand, are you 'hanging around' with the people that you should be or do I have to ground you? You should be surrounding yourself with people who tick at least one of the following broad boxes: you need them or they need you, you like them and spending time with them makes you feel good about yourself, them and life in general, or there is synergy in your relationship, where you can achieve things by being together that you couldn't if you weren't.

Now I reckon that there are a fair few people who fit into one of those three rather large categories, but there will be some who don't. Think for a moment about the people who you currently are surrounding yourself with, and if you want to get clarity on who those people are, just consider the last month of your life and which people have heard your voice or seen your face the most. Are they the ones who should be the answer to the question that I've posed, and if not, who do you need to spend less time with to create the space for those who require more regular access?

I've always believed that you should surround yourself with people who make you feel good about yourself, and wave goodbye to those who like to put you down, either to your face or behind your back. Who makes you feel good about yourself, there when you need them to put a spring in your step, a smile on your face and acts as a reminder of just how fine a person you actually are? Yet life isn't all hedonistic, obliterating the mundane and mediocre for a 24/7 foam party, there are people out there who need us or even depend on us. Are you spending enough time with these people – are you surrounding them?

One of the weekly tasks that always irritates me is filling up the car with fuel – it always feels such a waste of time. Ridiculous really when you consider that it never takes more than five minutes and by completing the task it enables me to get from A to B wherever the geographical version of those two letters are. We need fuel in our tank and we need certain people in our lives who perform a similar task. They're absolutely vital to ensure the smooth running of our daily lives and we need to surround ourselves with them, and forgetting to do so will leave you spluttering in the slow lane, regretting your decision. They're no waste of time and no irritation and you know it, so consider for a moment those people that you might take for granted and what you might do to correct this.

This question has two parts, so on to the second part and 'what' should you be surrounding yourself with? Wherever you are reading, stop and take a look around you – what can you see? What's on your desk, by your armchair or at the side of your bed? Now cast the net a bit wider and consider what you have been surrounding yourself with over the last few weeks. Think of the books, the bottles and the bags and reflect on the contents – happy with your choices and purchases? Are those items that are close by designed to make your life easier or are they inadvertently slowing you down or distracting you from what you could or should be doing?

I'm surrounded by holiday brochures at the moment and that feels good. Sitting in my office as I look left and right I am reminded how beautiful my loved ones are as they smile back at me via the camera lens. I like this game, surveying my surroundings I'm 2-0 up in no time! Then I look at my bin and see the variety of empty wrappers of sweets and bars that claim to be healthy but aren't. I need to add a fruit bowl to my surroundings, and while I'm at it I reckon I need to drink more water and should have it close by at all times. Two additions to my office that would help me in my quest for a healthier life.

As you look around you what should you be bringing into closer proximity? So my score after only a couple of minutes is two all and right on cue another 'who' surfaces, as my dog (and fourth daughter) shuffles in to say hello and helps me restore the lead. Now I don't want to alienate the half of my readers that are of a more feline persuasion but Ella is like the Mars bar advert of yesteryear for me – helping me work, rest and play. Who or what if you were to surround yourself with them would tick one, two or all three of those boxes? So there you have it, surround yourself with dogs and all will be well in your world!

49. WHICH PART OF YOUR BODY DO YOU NEED TO PAY MORE ATTENTION TO?

Some questions in this book are more open-ended than others and this is one of them, with so many variables as to how you might answer. I don't care which direction you take and what answer you give, just let your head, heart, gut or feet take you wherever they need to go. You see, four body parts in one sentence, our body parts guide us more than you might think they do.

At a recent client conference I was delivering a keynote, designed to help leaders increase the effectiveness of their decision making, and during the fun I asked the assembled audience to stand up and complete the following sentence in one word: 'I tend to make most decisions with my blank'. Blank is the word that needs replacing with your own ending you understand, so what would yours be? I then asked all those whose word was not a part of the body to sit down. A guy right at the front in the middle sat down so I asked him if he would mind sharing his word. "Easy," he said, "I tend to make most decisions with my wife." Good answer sir! Why didn't I think of that one?

The large majority of the group remained standing and when asked to provide their responses, the most popular word was head. Several said gut and there was the occasional heart. This in itself was a defining moment for the community as it became apparent that the task was deemed more important than the relationship, the head was more important than the heart, and thoughts were more important than feelings.

In his work on emotional intelligence Dan Goleman wrote 'No creature can fly with just one wing. Gifted leadership occurs where heart and head – feeling and thought – meet. These are the two wings that allow a leader to soar'. As I shared these words with the group it gave them plenty to contemplate. What does your response give you cause to think about, and of the head, heart, gut triumvirate which one might you neglect to listen to more than you should?

You see, this chapter isn't quite so cosmetic as you first thought is it? Although that's fine too if that's where you want to go. If you're looking at the bags under your eyes or the quality of your fingernails, then maybe you've made the decision to spend some of your hard-earned money on pampering yourself. And why not, we could all do with some of that every once in a while. Two of my favourite days every year are when my wife and I head off to a remote spa where I am reminded that my body is indeed a temple.

Or perhaps the reasons are slightly more tenuous; how about clearing your ears out so you can listen more effectively, getting your eyes tested so you can see further than the end of your nose, or working those muscles of yours so you can carry a bit more weight on your shoulders? Forgive me for being slightly tongue in cheek with my suggestions (and there's another two for you to consider!).

How do you feel about your body? If you're like me and most people I know it's probably a mix of the good, the bad and the ugly. I'm happy with my eyes and my legs if that doesn't sound too vain. I've been pretty open with you throughout this book so there's no reason to change now. My knee is playing up, I'm constantly striving to reduce my waist, and yes I've found my answer – my teeth! I need to pay more attention to my teeth. Since I was about 12 the number of teeth in my mouth has reduced and those that I'm left with need a bit of love and money sending their way. Which parts of your body do you need to offer a spot of TLC before it's too late?

I'm not saying that we all need to go in search of the body beautiful, ready to grace the covers of magazines with edited photographs depicting a perfection that is as unreal as it is unachievable. I'm just putting it out there that there is probably something between your head and your feet that you might need to consider focusing on. So far the components that I have cited are all visible to others – they look at you and think 'great ears' or 'what nice fingers you've got' but what about what lies beneath, anything inside that you might need to give some thought to?

No one glances you up and down and says 'hey, cracking liver you've got there' or 'great set of kidneys mate' and so out of sight may well mean out of mind but pay attention to them we must. Do you know how your internal organs are getting along? I recently had a blood test as part of keeping a close eye on my blood pressure, something I have a couple of times a year. This time something different happened though, because I received a phone call from the doctor's surgery a few days after the test. Apparently they wanted to see me.

When I entered the doctor's room he politely asked the reason for my visit to which I replied, "Dunno, you asked to see me." He turned to his screen, scrolled down for a few seconds before asking, "How much do you drink?" Apparently, whatever people answer to this loaded question the doctors double to get an accurate response, so I thought of an answer and he doubled it before telling me in a forthright manner, "You drink too much and as a result your liver is showing signs of damage. Cut down your drinking or cut down your life expectancy." He couldn't have put it any simpler than that, and I left the room with clarity and concern. So reduce it I did and subsequent tests have shown that my liver has returned to normal, whatever normal is.

What tests should you be having to ensure that the life you lead is healthy, happy and long? Listen to your body, pay attention to it – it's the only one you've got.

50. WHAT SHOULD BE ON YOUR NOT TO-DO LIST?

How's that to-do list coming along? Are you ticking them off one by one, basking in the glory of being well on your way to completing every task that is on there for the seventh consecutive day? Phew, thank goodness it's not just me, otherwise I'd be getting a complex!

Cards on the table, I must create about 20 to-do lists a day, constantly revising and refreshing them to account for the slow progress on the original list that was created as soon as I was showered and breakfasted, only slightly revised from the one that was created just prior to the heading upstairs to get some shut-eye. Here's my issue, I clutter my day with all sorts of nonsense that I shouldn't be doing, a smorgasbord of tasks that are neither urgent nor important but are, it has to be said, fairly easy. I focus on those issues that can either wait another day, be passed elsewhere or just not be done at all because in all reality they are just not that important. They should be on my not to-do list.

What should be on your not to-do list? What are those topics that occupy your time, effort and energy that quite frankly are not worth it? They stop you from focusing on the things that matter – those tasks that add value, give you a sense of achievement or that you actually enjoy doing.

If it helps, in writing this chapter I thought about my own not to-do list and here are some 'agenda items' that found their way on there. Number one: stop writing so many to-do lists! This one is a real issue for me. No day is off limits for a frequently revised list – weekdays, weekends, holidays, even Christmas Day! The last time I didn't write a to-do list was probably in my teens. Now I'm not saying that they are taboo, but I need to reduce the amount of times I rip up a previously created list for an updated one, I'm sure five a day would suffice. I'm becoming increasingly conscious of the fact that I am left deflated by the fact that I don't complete the list that I set myself even though I invariably bite off more than I can chew. What should be on your not to-do list because it puts you under unnecessary pressure?

Number two on my list: stop doing the things that excite me yet at the same time distract me. I love holidays and in return for working my socks off for eight weeks in a row I ensure that I have a break – near or far, long or short – at the end of that two-month burst. The problem is that these breaks become all-consuming and I spend a disproportionate amount of time researching the place, the flights, the hotels, restaurants, you name it I research it. And when I'm doing that I'm not getting on with the tasks that pay for such adventures. What do you need to add to your developing not to-do list that fits into the category 'enjoyable but distracting'?

Another one that is on my list relates to emails. For some reason I pride myself on replying to every email almost immediately. As far as I'm aware there is no current business award on offer for such a category, and whilst it is an admirable quality on topics that require such a swift response due to their urgency and importance, it's fair to say that not all of my inbox is populated with emails that fit both criteria. So added to my list is not to attempt to answer all emails within the same minute that I received them. They just put me off what I was in the middle of or give me an excuse to procrastinate on those tasks where I was looking for an excuse to do exactly that. Which takes me to number four: stop procrastinating. Stop putting all the tasks that I enjoy doing most at the front of my day, ensuring as a result that the meaty, challenging tasks just get shunted from one to-do list to the next.

That's enough of mine, I've given you four that you may or may not be able to relate to, steal them if you wish and add them to yours, but now you get my drift what should you be adding to yours? What are those things that you do that stop you from doing what really matters? What are those behaviours that you display that you'd rather not, and can you find a way to give them a place in your top ten? What are those distractions, demotivators or derailers that would be best passed to someone else or passed over altogether?

The ones I mentioned might sound like they have quite a business focus, but that need not be the case. Think about your home for a moment and those who share it with you – what should you not be doing? Whether it be not using mobile phones in bed, going to sleep on an argument or other principles that don't have anything to do with what goes on in the bedroom, these make good additions to that not-to list. Nothing is out of bounds, it's your list after all! So feel liberated to add 'making the house tidy before the cleaner arrives' and such like to it – make it personal, varied and yours.

If you're thinking to yourself that this all sounds a tad negative and wondering why you can't frame things in a more positive manner, I'm with you to a certain extent but the reality is that these are the things that get in the way of all the positive intent that consumes your to-do list. Rather than create one list instead of the other, have two. To-do or not to-do, that is the question.

Over to you now, you've got a list to create, or at least I hope you have. Unless that is you've put 'create a not to-do list' on your list. Well, if you have you've done what I asked so my work is complete, but I reckon you can do better than that if you really tried!

51. WHAT JOURNEY SHOULD YOU BE EMBARKING ON?

Few things broaden the mind like travel. I feel truly blessed to have been able to work around the world, and as a result experience different cultures, climates and challenges. Technology has ensured that in some ways we live in a small world, connected to different parts of the planet, yet geographically it's the same size as it always was. Get your map out, it's rather large this Earth thing that we all populate.

Now not everyone has my wanderlust and I accept that, but the question remains, where should you be going that either you have never previously been to or haven't frequented for a while? Near or far, east or west, where would you benefit from travelling to in search of your true north, or your Auntie Elsie for that matter? Where have you always wanted to go but never quite reached? Whose posts have you liked whilst secretly feeling a little bit envious, thinking to yourself 'I'd love to go there'? What's stopping you? If the journey itself is the cause of procrastination or concern then look beyond planes, trains and automobiles and think about the destination. No pain no gain they say – are you prepared to take that route to get to where you want to get to?

My youngest daughter recently ventured to Machu Picchu, taking the proper path, walking through challenging conditions in order to feel the sense of achievement that goes with the view when you get there. My middle daughter explored Australia before I did and my eldest has travelled more than once to her favourite country India, uncharted territory for me. They're all at it, the Jones girls and I absolutely love it!

Where would give you a thrill, a new experience, a sense of contentment, or maybe closure? If the answers are all in the travels of my kids then I don't believe you – get your own answers, and while you're giving them consideration let me just clarify that they don't all have to require visas, inoculations and flights that arrive on a different day than they departed.

Think for a moment about the last places that you visited for the first time – a town, city, park, beach, house or restaurant. Our lives are populated with first-time experiences and virgin territory. On a recent visit to Italy we returned to one of our favourite cities of the world, Bologna. I'd thoroughly recommend that you pay it a visit at some point for too many reasons than this chapter allows me to go into, but while we used familiar surroundings as our base, we boarded the train to four cities that were all within 75 minutes of our home for the week.

By doing this we were able to experience the history of Ferrara, the peace of Ravenna, the affluence of Parma and the piazzas of Modena. OK, so my three travelling companions might have been glad of the rest when we returned home but they wouldn't have missed these places that were on our doorstep for the world. Where's on your doorstep that you should be exploring?

Before you ask, Bologna was extremely cheap to get to, the same cost as a trip to the cinema that we had last Saturday night. The flight time was two hours, the same amount of time that many people I know spend commuting every day. Whatever hurdles you put in your way for such trips there is a solution, but maybe you don't want to hear it.

Our Italian adventure was a holiday but not all journeys require a bucket and spade be packed. I mentioned a few of the reasons earlier so let's give them some consideration. Living as I do in Cheshire in the north-west of England I am practically equidistant between the two northern powerhouses of Manchester and Liverpool. The rivalry is intense but one thing that connects them is the Manchester Ship Canal, built to give Manchester access to the sea that Liverpool is built around.

I've never travelled on this stretch of water but have recently seen that there are boat trips from one end of the canal to the other with the obligatory commentary to explain all the places and landmarks en route. We're going on this trip, but it's no holiday. The closest part of the canal is eight miles from our house so we hardly need to pack a suitcase. We'll be back in time to feed the dog (she's not allowed on this trip sadly). What would your version of this journey be and what's stopping you from having such a local explore?

What about that contentment and closure that I mentioned? It's always an emotional moment when television captures war veterans heading back to shores where they lost comrades. As we walk the coastal path of south-west England we are drawn to the plaques on benches, placed in memory of loved ones acknowledging their favourite spot. For some they provide closure, for others they provide closeness. Where should you be going to be closer to those people, places or memories that you hold dear? Travel takes us further but it also brings us closer.

On my travels more often than not I enter the arrivals halls at airports around the world to no welcome party. I head to the taxi rank or train station ready to embark on the final leg of my journey. Yet as I do I'm aware that I am surrounded by people being reunited with loved ones – the laughter, tears, balloons and banners stir my own emotions even though these are people that

I've never seen before and will most likely never see again. Who is waiting for you to come through the arrivals hall so they can hold you for the first time in too long? Who should you be visiting regardless of whether you need to head overseas or across town to renew acquaintances?

As Ibn Battuta said, "Travelling leaves you speechless, then turns you into a storyteller." He said this in the 14th century and there were no budget airlines in those days. So whether it's the places or the people that you want to see when you get there, where is 'there' and what steps do you need to take to move in the right direction? What are you waiting for? Get on your bike, or whatever mode of transport will get you there swiftly and safely. There's a story out there that's waiting for you to find the ending to.

52. IF YOU WERE TO PAINT A PICTURE OF HOW YOU WANT YOUR WORLD TO BE, WHAT WOULD BE IN THE CENTRE?

It's no self-limiting belief, I'm hopeless when it comes to painting or drawing. In fact, if one of these questions was 'what is the one thing in your life that you are hopeless at?' then I've found my response, but then the book probably wouldn't sell as many copies as I would like if it was populated with such negativity! So leave that one for now if you will and focus on the one that was originally posed.

During a conference that I was speaking at a number of years ago there was a breakout session conducted by someone far more adept in this area than anyone else I've ever met, a mighty decent and talented chap called Louis Parsons. Balancing his two roles as a stunning artist and accomplished speaker and coach, he took the audience through what he called a 'Vision Scaping' process, allowing their creativity to shine as they defined and articulated their vision.

As I took part in the session, using only my fingers (as instructed) to create my work of 'art', it struck me that this was the first time that I had painted something that was neither a wall nor a door since my school days. Whilst the finished product might not have sold many copies the significance to me was profound, so much so that I had it framed and it has remained in my home office ever since. In order to look forward he asked us to look back, reflecting on that one defining moment when we felt most alive. My finger painting depicts my first walk with my wife – I bet you're disappointed with that aren't you, yet that was the memory that came to me as I reflected on the questions that he posed and it conveyed a sense of new beginnings and rejuvenation.

Imagine that you are about to embark on a similar experience but I'll allow you to use a brush if you think that your fingers aren't suitable for the task. This time, however, look forward to the future while drawing on the past and present as you do so. In your picture what would you like to be in the centre? Is there one single thought, feeling, belief or value that might hold centre stage? Or maybe it's something altogether more tangible or even materialistic (who am I to judge, it's your artwork after all). Rather than a 'what' is it a 'who'? And how does this painting of how you want your world to be actually compare to how your world currently is? What would be in the current version that you would like to whitewash and paint over, and what would be on the desired alternative that has either been missing for some time or never been there at all?

Only by identifying those two stakes in the ground can you begin to plan how to make moves in the right direction. For instance, if you have a hammock in the centre of your painting, surrounded by an idyllic tranquil garden yet currently you can't remember when you last had five minutes to yourself, then you might need to consider the first steps to making such a transition. The thought behind my question isn't merely for you to create an unrealistic dream, more to gain clarity on what is really important to you and put it front and centre of everything that you do.

Some responses will undoubtedly be more prevalent than others when it comes to answering a question such as this. If you're in a long-term relationship, it's hoped that your partner of choice would be high on your list and so would any children that you may have created together. Friends and family would probably be added to the mix, so in no time at all your creation might have the appearance of a house party, with a sea of faces looking back at you. But what if faces weren't allowed on there – what would the words be that you were attempting to represent pictorially?

He had a good range of colours did Louis, but my creation was primarily composed of three of them: the yellow of the sun, the blue of the water and the green of the grass. As you envisage your painting what colours are shining through and why? If you were to add a touch more colour to your world what do you need to focus on and what would it be representing?

As always throughout this book I am drawn to answer my own question as I pose it to you. As I consider the centre of what I would like my world to be I am compelled to reach for the previously untouched red paint and create probably the one symbol that I doodle more than any other and probably the only one that would be recognisable by you or anyone else – a heart. Is there a symbol or an emblem that might form the centrepiece of your work? A heart can signify many things but for me it is the combination of love, purpose and health. There are times when I focus on only two of these and take my eye off the remaining one so today my art work would be heart work with three roads leading to the centre.

I must get in touch with Louis, it's been a good few years since we last met over a coffee to discuss how we might collaborate more yet we never did so. His work is so different from mine yet in many ways so aligned. I'm going to ask him to read this chapter and make him aware of the impact that his 45-minute session had on me. He didn't make me a better artist but he made me refocus on what was important and that can only ever be a good thing. Perhaps now is the time for me to look to work more closely with him.

What is it time for you to focus on that you have often considered but never actually made much progress on? Whether you choose to create something and frame it or just consider the question and write your thoughts down is up to you – it's your picture and it's your centre. It's your world too. No one else's work will be quite the same.

REVIEW

So there you go, 52 questions that have cajoled, nudged and nurdled you into contemplating what's important, who's important and why, and what you should be focusing more and less on now that you've taken the time and trouble to read this book from start to finish.

But the questions haven't finished quite yet (you didn't really think they had now did you?). I'd like you to take some time out, review some of the notes and actions that you've created and spot some of the common themes that emerge. Who were those people that you thought of most, regardless of the question? I expect that there's probably a top ten waiting to be created somewhere, populated with those names that sprang to mind time and time again as you strived to give your considered response. As you reflect on these names what aspect of your world do they primarily populate and how content are you with the way that these relationships currently operate?

After so many questions I've no doubt that you have a whole host of actions that you are ready to deploy that will change them for the better, and hopefully you haven't waited until you've reached The End before putting some of them into practice.

What's going to change about you as a result of the time that you've spent interacting with this book? It was never the intention to create a new you, more a revised, updated version to go along the ever-changing world in which you go about your business. What recurring issues came to the surface, too often to ignore and regular enough to provide clarity on how important and pressing they are? Who will notice and what will they notice? What will people say differently about you once your positive intentions have been carried out?

It might not be you who is going to change but it might be the world around you – the situations that you find yourself in. What are some of those actions that you need to put into place, the ones that don't change who you are, more where you are, and when? What's going to be simpler, easier and clearer as you move forward and how are you going to spend your time?

If you've gone through this book in the way that I had hoped (and you hoped when you made the decision to buy it), I reckon that there have been many decisions made – about you, your relationships, your focus and your health and wellbeing. And as you consider the actions the likelihood is that a handful of them are bigger, brighter and bolder than the others. That focused fistful at the forefront of your mind – you may or may not have been aware of them before embarking on this journey, but now you are where you are, procrastination is no longer an option. Well it's an option because we always have options, but both you and I know that it's not an option that you're going to take. The time is now.

How do you feel now that you've reflected, reacted and ultimately responded to the equivalent of one question a week for a whole year of your life? Are you glad it's over or are you expectantly looking forward to the sequel? That might depend on the questions that were posed in book two, because no doubt some would have been more challenging for you whereas others were a walk in the park. Yet the person to whom you recommend this book will have their own perception on which were a breeze and which had them heading to a darkened room, and it is unlikely to be the same as yours.

Go back to the contents page at the start of the book where all 52 questions are shown for a couple of minutes. As you take a look at them all, reflect on which ones you found most difficult to answer and why. Which were most timely, and which were less relevant? Which one do you think might be different now if you were to answer it again, even though it wasn't that long ago that you responded to it? I didn't say you could only answer it once so if you want to go back, then be my guest!

What questions were you glad that I didn't ask you and why? Whatever they were, you're off the hook for now. It's time to give yourself a little break, from me anyway. Keep asking yourself questions though, keep challenging yourself, show a curiosity about the world around you, in the people that surround you and in yourself. You are one interesting and complex person, so do as Einstein suggested – 'never stop questioning' as you strive to get deeper inside your head and heart.

In this book I've called on you to consider your whole self and in the process you've been complimentary and you've been critical but I want to leave you with one more thing before we say our goodbyes. I'd like to end on a positive and I'm going to keep it simple. Grab a pen one last time and write down six qualities that you like about yourself. Once you've created them put them into one short sentence that begins with the words 'I am a' and ends however you want it to end.

Some of these attributes will have been there since you were a child, some might have developed in more recent times, and some you might only have become aware of since you picked up these pages for the first time. The common denominator is that they are all you and the thoughts of the person that matters most. You. Don't lose sight of the commitments, promises and actions you have identified but don't forget that you are building on some pretty impressive foundations.

Thanks for sticking with it, now give yourself a pat on the back. I hope you agree with me that there were some searching questions posed. As for the answers, I reckon that some of them are rather good too, no question about it.

ABOUT THE AUTHOR

Mike Jones is Managing Director of Momentum (People Development) Ltd and has nearly 30 years' experience in the Learning and Development industry, helping individuals, teams and organisations understand what makes them tick.

He has delivered at conferences and facilitated workshops in over 35 countries and his passion, energy and wit have made him a highly sought after speaker to groups large and small.

Equally adept at both design and delivery, Mike spent 15 years as Global Head of Delivery at Insights, a world-leading people development organisation, where he designed a wide range of innovative products and solutions that were experienced by thousands around the world.

Mike's love of travel ensures that wherever his business ventures take him, there's an adventure that accompanies it. When not travelling, he recharges his batteries by following football and cricket with a passion and taking Ella, his labrador, on long walks.

NOTES

NOTES

NOTES

NOTES